BILINGUAL TALES FOR KIDS: JAPANESE EDITION

25 Stories in Japanese and English

Mei Nakamura

This book was designed using resources from
www.freepik.com

polyglotpublications@gmail.com

Contents

Introduction

Welcome to Bilingual Tales for Kids: Japanese Edition, a captivating series designed to guide you on a linguistic journey like no other. Whether you're a language enthusiast, a curious learner, or someone who simply loves stories, this collection will take you on a thrilling adventure through the realms of language and literature.

In this unique book series, we combine the power of storytelling with the art of language acquisition. By immersing yourself in 25 carefully selected short stories, you will embark on an engaging path to mastering a new language. Each story is presented in both your native language and the target language, allowing you to effortlessly transition between the two as you explore the world of words and cultures.

Our approach recognizes the inherent connection between language and narrative. By exposing you to narratives in multiple languages, Bilingual Tales for Kids fosters a deep understanding of language structure, vocabulary, idiomatic expressions, and cultural nuances. As you progress through the stories, you'll notice your comprehension and fluency growing organically, as if absorbed through the very fabric of the tales themselves.

The stories in Bilingual Tales for Kids: Japanese Edition are carefully crafted to captivate your imagination and provoke thoughtful reflection. From heartwarming tales of friendship and love to thrilling adventures in far-off lands, each story presents a rich tapestry of emotions, characters, and settings that will transport you to new horizons.

Within these pages, you'll find a seamless integration of two languages, inviting you to compare and contrast linguistic elements effortlessly. As you delve into the stories, take note of the similarities and differences between the languages, and allow the connections to deepen your grasp of both.

Bilingual Tales for Kids: Japanese Edition is not just a series of stories; it is an invitation to discover the profound joy of learning a new language through the magic of storytelling. It embraces the belief that language is best acquired when it becomes an integral part of our everyday experiences. By embedding language within the narrative fabric of these tales, we hope to ignite your passion for language learning and spark your curiosity to explore the world of words.

So, embark on this linguistic adventure with us. Let Bilingual Tales for Kids: Japanese Edition be your guide as you uncover the treasures hidden within the pages of each story. Whether you're starting from scratch or seeking to refine your language skills, this series will accompany you on an exciting voyage toward fluency, one tale at a time.

Get ready to open your mind, open your heart, and open the door to a world of languages and stories.

Happy reading, and bon voyage!

The Bilingual Tales for Kids Team

User Guide

Welcome to the User Guide for Bilingual Tales for Kids: Japanese Edition. This guide is designed to help you navigate through the book series and make the most of your language learning experience. Here, you will find valuable tips, suggestions, and instructions to enhance your journey through the stories.

1. Getting Started:

- Familiarize yourself with the structure of the book. Each story is presented with the native language on one page and the target language on the facing page.

2. Setting Goals:

- Determine your language learning goals. Are you aiming for conversational proficiency, reading comprehension, or overall fluency? Clearly defining your objectives will help you stay focused and motivated throughout the series.

3. Reading Strategies:

- Start with the native language version to grasp the storyline and become familiar with the characters, plot, and themes.
- Once you have a basic understanding of the story, move on to the target language version. Read through the text, focusing on comprehension rather than word-for-word translation.
- Utilize context clues, sentence structure, and illustrations to aid your understanding of unfamiliar words or phrases.
- Highlight or underline new vocabulary and phrases. Create

a personalized vocabulary list or flashcards to reinforce your learning.
- Practice reading aloud to improve pronunciation and rhythm.

4. Comparative Analysis:

- Compare the native language and target language versions of each story. Pay attention to the similarities and differences in sentence structure, word usage, and cultural references.
- Reflect on how language choices affect the overall tone and meaning of the story.
- Take note of idiomatic expressions or colloquialisms unique to the target language. This will deepen your understanding of the language's cultural context.

5. Engaging with the Material:

- Immerse yourself in the stories. Let the narratives captivate your imagination and evoke emotions.
- Engage in discussions with language partners or fellow learners. Share your interpretations of the stories and exchange language learning strategies.
- Write summaries or reflections on each story in the target language. This will reinforce your language skills and provide opportunities for self-expression.

6. Progress Monitoring:

- Track your progress by periodically reviewing previous stories. Observe how your comprehension and language skills have improved over time.
- Celebrate milestones and achievements along your language learning journey. Recognize the progress you have made and use it as motivation to continue.

7. Additional Resources:

- Supplement your learning with external resources such as language learning apps, online courses, or language exchange programs.
- Seek out native speakers or language tutors for practice and guidance.
- Utilize language dictionaries, grammar guides, and online forums for additional support.
- Remember, Bilingual Tales for Kids: Japanese Edition is a flexible learning tool. Customize your approach to suit your learning style and needs. The more actively you engage with the stories, the more rewarding and effective your language learning experience will be.

Enjoy the enchanting stories, embrace the beauty of language, and embark on a remarkable journey to bilingualism!

The Bilingual Tales for Kids Team

Meiji Shrine

In the heart of Tokyo, nestled amidst the **bustling** streets and towering skyscrapers, stood a place of serene beauty—the Meiji Shrine. Its grand entrance welcomed visitors into a world where time seemed to slow down, and the past melded seamlessly with the present. On a warm summer's day, as the sunlight filtered through the lush green **canopy**, a young woman named Ayumi found herself drawn to the tranquil allure of the shrine. With a heart filled with curiosity, she embarked on a journey of discovery. As she stepped onto the gravel path, Ayumi sensed the weight of history around her. The **towering** torii gate loomed ahead, marking the transition from the mundane to the sacred. She breathed in deeply, feeling the air change, carrying with it the essence of tradition. Ayumi followed the winding trail, guided by the enchanting melody of wind chimes that swayed gently in the **breeze**. The surrounding trees whispered secrets of the past, and she listened intently, letting her imagination soar.

With each step, Ayumi delved further into the realm of the Meiji era. She envisioned the shrine in its prime—a vibrant hub of culture and **spirituality**. The echoes of ancient rituals danced in her mind as she glimpsed priests in ceremonial robes,

明治神宮

東京の中心部、喧騒と高層ビル群に囲まれた場所に、静謐な美しさをたたえた明治神宮があります。その壮大なエントランスは、訪れる人々を、時間がゆっくりと流れ、過去と現在がシームレスに融合した世界へと導いてくれます。ある夏の日、緑の**木漏れ日の中**、若い女性アユミはその静謐な魅力に引き込まれた。好奇心でいっぱいの彼女は、発見の旅に出た。砂利道に足を踏み入れると、あゆみは歴史の重みを感じた。鳥居が**そびえ立ち**、日常から聖なるものへと変化していく。深く息を吸い込むと、空気が変化し、伝統のエッセンスを運んでくるのを感じた。あゆみは、**風に**揺れる風鈴の音に誘われるように、曲がりくねった道を進んでいった。周囲の木々は過去の秘密をささやき、彼女は耳を澄まし、想像を膨らませた。

歩を進めるごとに、あゆみは明治の世界に入り込んでいく。文化や**精神が息づく**神社の全盛期を思い描いた。祭服に身を包んだ神職の声が響き、古代の儀式の響きが脳裏をよぎる。中庭に近づくと、子供たちがかくれんぼに**夢中になっているの**が目に入った。その笑い声は木の葉のざわめきに混じって、まるで昔の楽しい気分を呼び起こすかのようだ。その様子を微笑ましく見ていると、神社に**漂う**活気と深いつながりを感じる。そんな中、あゆみは小さな池を見つけた。その池の水面には、紺碧の空が映し出されていた。その池の水面が紺碧の空に映える。

their chants resonating through the air. As she approached the inner courtyard, Ayumi noticed a group of children **engrossed** in a game of hide-and-seek. Their laughter mingled with the rustling leaves, as if echoing the joyous spirits of the past. Smiling, she watched them, feeling a profound connection to the lively energy that **permeated** the shrine. In the midst of her reverie, Ayumi stumbled upon a small pond, its crystal-clear waters reflecting the **azure** sky above. She crouched down, mesmerized by the sight. The ripples created by her touch seemed to carry her wishes to the sacred realm.

Lost in her thoughts, Ayumi noticed a elderly man sitting nearby, his face etched with **wisdom**. Curiosity piqued, she approached him **cautiously**. He smiled warmly and beckoned her to sit beside him. "Welcome, young one," he said, his voice melodic and soothing. "The Meiji Shrine is a gateway to the past, a place where dreams and reality intertwine. It holds the **memories** of those who came before us, and their spirit lives on." Ayumi listened intently, her heart brimming with gratitude. The man's words resonated deeply within her, reminding her of the power of **heritage** and the importance of cherishing the present.

そんな中、あゆみは近くに座っている老人に目を留めた。その老人は**知恵のある**顔をしていた。好奇心を刺激された彼女は、**慎重に彼に近づいた**。すると、老人は温かく微笑み、自分の横に座るように手招きした。「ようこそ、若い人」と、彼の声はメロディックで心地よい。「明治神宮は過去への入り口であり、夢と現実が交錯する場所です。明治神宮には先人たちの**記憶があり**、その魂は今も生き続けています。あゆみは、感謝の気持ちで胸がいっぱいになりながら、じっと耳を傾けた。その言葉に、あゆみは深く共鳴し、**遺産の力**、今を大切にすることの大切さを感じた。

Comprehension Questions

1. Where is the Meiji Shrine located?

2. What impression does the grand entrance of the shrine create for visitors?

3. What attracted Ayumi to the shrine on that particular day?

4. How does Ayumi feel as she steps onto the gravel path?

5. What does the towering torii gate symbolize?

6. What guided Ayumi along the winding trail?

7. What does Ayumi imagine as she delves further into the shrine's realm?

8. What did Ayumi observe happening in the inner courtyard?

9. How did Ayumi feel while watching the children in the shrine?

10. What did Ayumi notice about the small pond she stumbled upon?

理解度チェック問題

1. 明治神宮はどこにあるのですか？
2. 神社の壮大なエントランスは、訪れる人にどんな印象を与えているのでしょうか。
3. あの日、あゆみはどんな思いで神社に足を運んだのだろう。
4. 砂利道に足を踏み入れたあゆみは、どんな気持ちなのだろう。
5. そびえ立つ鳥居は何を象徴しているのでしょうか。
6. 曲がりくねった道を歩むあゆみを導いてくれたものは何だったのか。
7. 神社の領域をさらに掘り下げていく中で、あゆみは何を想像するのか。
8. あゆみさんは、中庭で何が起こっているのかを観察したのでしょうか。
9. 神社の子どもたちを見ながら、あゆみはどんな気持ちだったのだろう。
10. 偶然見つけた小さな池で、あゆみはどんなことに気づいたのだろう。

Hanafuda

In a small village nestled at the foot of a **mountain**, there lived a young girl named Emi. Her days were filled with the vibrant colors of nature and the gentle songs of birds. But deep inside, Emi longed for something more—a sense of adventure and mystery. One summer **afternoon**, while exploring the attic of her grandmother's house, Emi stumbled upon an old wooden box. Curiosity ignited within her, and she carefully lifted the lid, revealing a treasure trove of hanafuda cards. Their intricate designs and delicate hues fascinated her. Emi's grandmother appeared, a smile lighting up her **weathered** face. "Ah, the hanafuda," she said softly. "They carry the stories of our ancestors, Emi. Would you like me to teach you how to play?" Eagerly, Emi nodded, and her grandmother **patiently** explained the rules of the ancient card game. As the sun dipped below the horizon, they settled down on a woven mat, arranging the cards before them.

With each game, Emi was transported to a different world—a realm where flowers bloomed with vibrant **intensity** and animals spoke in hushed **whispers**. The cards became her companions, guiding her through tales of love, nature, and myth. As the seasons changed, so did Emi. Her skill in playing

花札

山のふもとにある小さな村に、エミという名の少女が住んでいました。エミは、色鮮やかな自然と鳥のさえずりに包まれた日々を送っていました。しかし、エミは心の奥底で、もっと冒険やミステリーに憧れていました。ある夏の**午後**、祖母の家の屋根裏を探検していたエミは、古い木箱を偶然見つけました。好奇心に火がついたエミは、慎重に蓋を開けると、そこには宝物のような花札があった。その複雑な絵柄と繊細な色合いに、エミは心を奪われた。すると、恵美の祖母が現れ、その**老けた顔**に笑みを浮かべた。「ああ、花札ね」と祖母は優しく言った。「花札には先祖の物語が詰まっているんだよ、エミちゃん。弾き方を教えてあげようか？ 祖母は根気よくそのルールを教えてくれた。太陽が地平線に沈むと、二人は布製のマットの上に腰を下ろし、カードを並べた。

花々が**鮮やかに咲き誇り**、動物たちが**ひそひそと話す**世界。カードはエミの仲間になり、愛や自然、神話などの物語を案内してくれる。季節が変われば、絵美も変わる。花札の腕前も上達し、カードに隠された秘密をより深く知るようになった。桜は人生の**儚さ**を、紅葉は変容を、鶴は幸運と長寿を象徴しているのである。ある日、村に一人の語り部（ストーリーテラー）がやってきた。エミは、花札の魅力に取りつかれ、その魅力を伝えたいと思った。エミは花札の魅力を伝えたいと思った。

"ああ、若き日のエミさん "と、ほのかな**感嘆の声を上げた**。「花札には物語だけでなく、持つ人の想像力を解き放つ力がある。現実と**空想**のギャップを埋める力があるのです。語り部の言葉に触発された恵美は、花札を手が

hanafuda grew, and she delved deeper into the secrets hidden within the cards. She discovered that each suit held a symbolic power—the cherry blossoms symbolized the **ephemeral** nature of life, the maple leaves represented transformation, and the cranes embodied luck and longevity. One day, a traveling storyteller visited the village. His tales of distant lands and mythical **creatures** fascinated Emi, and she couldn't resist the urge to share her newfound passion for hanafuda. The storyteller listened intently, his eyes alight with curiosity.

"Ah, young Emi," he said, a hint of **admiration** in his voice. "The hanafuda cards hold not only stories but also the power to unlock the imagination of those who possess them. They have the ability to bridge the gap between reality and the **fantastical**." Inspired by the storyteller's words, Emi began to create her own tales using the hanafuda cards as her guide. She wove intricate stories of heroes and heroines, of **mythical** creatures and epic battles. The villagers gathered around her, captivated by the vivid worlds she conjured. As years passed, Emi's stories traveled far and wide, enchanting people from distant lands. The hanafuda cards became a **symbol** of her village, carrying with them the magic and wisdom of generations.

かりに自分なりの物語を作り始めた。英雄やヒロイン、**神話的な**生き物、壮大な戦いなど、複雑な物語を紡ぎ出していく。村人たちは彼女の周りに集まり、彼女の描く鮮やかな世界に魅了された。やがて、エミの物語は遠くまで伝わり、遠い国の人々も魅了するようになった。花札は村の**シンボルとなり**、何世代にもわたる魔法と知恵を携えていた。

Comprehension Questions

1. Where did Emi find the hanafuda cards?

2. What intrigued Emi about the hanafuda cards?

3. Who taught Emi how to play hanafuda?

4. What effect did playing hanafuda have on Emi's imagination?

5. What symbolic powers did Emi discover each suit of hanafuda cards held?

6. Who visited the village one day and sparked Emi's passion for storytelling?

7. How did the storyteller describe the power of the hanafuda cards?

8. How did Emi use the hanafuda cards to create her own stories?

9. How did the villagers respond to Emi's storytelling with the hanafuda cards?

10. What did the hanafuda cards become for Emi's village over the years?

理解度チェック問題

1. 恵美さんは花札をどこで見つけたのでしょうか?
2. 花札の何が恵美さんの興味をそそったのか?
3. 恵美さんに花札を教えたのは誰ですか?
4. 花札の演奏は、恵美さんの想像力にどんな影響を与えたのでしょうか。
5. エミは、花札の各スートがどのような象徴的な力を持っているのかを発見しました。
6. ある日、村を訪れ、エミの物語への情熱に火をつけたのは誰だったのか。
7. 語り部は花札の力をどのように表現したのでしょうか。
8. 恵美さんは花札をどのように使って、自分の物語を作っていったのでしょうか。
9. 花札を使った絵美さんの語りかけに、村人たちはどう反応したのでしょうか。
10. 花札は、長い年月を経て、エミの村にとってどんな存在になったのでしょうか。

Tadao Ando

In the heart of a bustling city, where the **cacophony** of
honking horns and hurried footsteps filled the air, there lived
a man named Tadao Ando. He was a master of architecture,
renowned for his ability to transform the concrete jungle into
harmonious spaces that awakened the soul. Tadao Ando's
journey began in humble beginnings. Growing up in Osaka,
he worked as a carpenter while nurturing his passion for
design. Determined to bring beauty and tranquility to urban
landscapes, he embarked on a quest to create spaces that would
touch people's hearts. One summer day, Tadao Ando found
himself in a small **coastal** town, drawn to its raw natural
beauty. He felt a deep connection to the rhythm of the ocean
and the vast **expanse** of the sky. Inspired, he made a promise
to himself—to build a structure that would capture the essence
of this place.

With unwavering determination, Tadao Ando began sketching
his vision—a **structure** that would seamlessly merge with the
surrounding landscape, celebrating the harmony of nature
and architecture. He envisioned a series of fluid lines, clean
geometric shapes, and a play of light and shadow that would
evoke a sense of peace and serenity. Months turned into years as

安藤忠雄

クラクションの音と慌ただしい足音が響く都会の真ん中に、安藤忠雄という男が住んでいた。彼は、コンクリートジャングルを**調和のとれた空間に変え**、魂を目覚めさせることで有名な建築の巨匠であった。安藤忠雄の旅は、地味なところから始まった。大阪で育った彼は、大工として働きながら、デザインへの情熱を育んでいきました。都会の風景に美しさと安らぎを与えたいという思いから、人の心に響く空間づくりの探求を始めたのです。ある夏の日、安藤忠雄は**海岸沿いの**小さな町で、その生々しい自然の美しさに惹かれました。海のリズムや広大な空の**広がり**に深いつながりを感じたのです。そして、この地のエッセンスを凝縮した建築物を作ろうと心に誓った。

安藤忠雄は、揺るぎない決意をもって、周囲の風景とシームレスに融合し、自然と建築が調和するような**建築物の構想**を描き始めました。それは、自然と建築の調和を図りながら、周囲の風景に溶け込むような建築物である。安藤忠雄が心血を注いで制作した作品は、月日が経ち、年月が経ちました。そして、ついに**完成したのが**、夕焼けの黄金色に輝くガラスとコンクリートの壮大な建造物だった。安藤忠雄の作品は、瞬く間に世間に広まりました。安藤忠雄の作品は瞬く間に広まり、その姿を一目見ようと多くの人が集まった。一歩足を踏み入れると、静寂に包まれ、時間がゆっくりと流れていく。海からの涼しい風と窓から差し込む**陽光が**、ミニマルなインテリアに魅惑的な輝きを与えている。

安藤忠雄は夢を実現した。彼の創造物は、混沌とした世

Tadao Ando poured his heart and soul into the creation. Finally, his **masterpiece** emerged—a magnificent glass and concrete structure, bathed in the golden hues of sunset. Word of Tadao Ando's creation spread like wildfire. Visitors flocked to witness the marvel firsthand. As they stepped inside, a hush fell over them, and time seemed to slow down. The cool breeze from the ocean mingled with the **sunlight** streaming through the windows, casting a mesmerizing glow on the minimalist interior.

Tadao Ando had achieved his dream—his creation had become a **sanctuary**, a refuge for weary souls seeking solace in a chaotic world. It became a place where one could connect with nature, find stillness, and rediscover the beauty within. The **accolades** poured in, but Tadao Ando remained humble, always striving for new challenges. His work spread across the globe, each project a testament to his dedication to creating spaces that nurtured the human spirit. But amidst the fame and recognition, Tadao Ando never forgot his roots. He continued to **inspire** young architects, sharing his knowledge and passion, reminding them of the profound impact **architecture** could have on people's lives. As the years passed, Tadao Ando's name became synonymous with innovation and beauty. His creations stood as testaments to his unwavering belief in the power of design to shape our surroundings and, in turn, shape our souls.

界の中で癒しを求める疲れた魂の避難所となった。自然とつながり、静寂を求め、内なる美を再発見できる場所となったのです。安藤忠雄は謙虚に、常に新しいことに挑戦し続けました。安藤忠雄の作品は世界中に広がり、そのどれもが、人間の精神を育む空間を創造するための彼の献身的な努力の証となっている。しかし、名声と評価の中で、安藤忠雄は決して自分のルーツを忘れることはなかった。**建築が**人々の生活に大きな影響を与えることを再認識させ、自らの知識と情熱を若い建築家たちに伝え続けました。年月が経つにつれ、安藤忠雄の名は、革新と美の代名詞となりました。安藤忠雄の作品は、私たちを取り巻く環境、ひいては私たちの魂を形作るデザインの力に対する彼の揺るぎない信念を証明するものとなっています。

Comprehension Questions

1. What was Tadao Ando renowned for?

2. Where did Tadao Ando grow up?

3. What was Tadao Ando's goal in his quest for creating spaces?

4. What inspired Tadao Ando to build a structure in a small coastal town?

5. How did Tadao Ando envision his structure merging with the surrounding landscape?

6. How did visitors react when they entered Tadao Ando's creation?

7. What did Tadao Ando's creation become for people seeking solace?

8. How did Tadao Ando respond to the accolades and recognition he received?

9. What did Tadao Ando continue to do despite his fame?

10. What did Tadao Ando believe about the impact of architecture on people's lives?

理解度チェック問題

1. 安藤忠雄はどんなことで有名だったのですか?

2. 安藤忠雄はどこで育ったのですか?

3. 安藤忠雄が目指した空間づくりとは?

4. 安藤忠雄が海岸沿いの小さな町に建築物を建てることになったきっかけは?

5. 安藤忠雄は、周囲の風景と融合する建築物をどのようにイメージしていたのでしょうか。

6. 安藤忠雄の作品に足を踏み入れたときの、来場者の反応は?

7. 安藤忠雄の創造は、癒しを求める人々にとってどのような存在になったのだろうか。

8. 安藤忠雄は、自分が受けた賞賛や評価をどのように受け止めていたのでしょうか。

9. 安藤忠雄は、名声を得てもなお、何をし続けたのでしょうか。

10. 安藤忠雄は、建築が人々の生活に与える影響について、どのように考えていたのだろうか。

Yakiniku

In the heart of a bustling city, amidst the **flickering** neon lights and the tantalizing aromas wafting through the streets, there existed a small, unassuming yakiniku restaurant. Its doors opened into a world of sizzling grills and a symphony of laughter and **conversation**. This was the place where friends gathered, families celebrated, and strangers became acquaintances over the shared joy of grilled meat. One summer evening, a young woman named Kaori found herself drawn to the enticing fragrance that drifted from the yakiniku **restaurant**. Curiosity piqued, she stepped inside, her senses immediately enveloped by the lively atmosphere. The sound of sizzling meat on the grill and the clinking of glasses filled the air, creating a symphony of **anticipation**.

Kaori was seated at a table adorned with a grill in its center, ready to embark on her yakiniku adventure. As the server brought a platter of marbled beef, **succulent** pork, and tender chicken, Kaori's mouth watered in anticipation. She carefully placed the pieces of meat on the grill, mesmerized by the sizzle and the aromatic smoke that rose into the air. With each bite, Kaori experienced a burst of flavors dancing on her palate. The **tender** beef melted like butter, releasing its rich and

焼肉

都会の真ん中で、ネオンが**きらめき**、香ばしい香りが漂う中、一軒の小さな焼肉屋があった。その扉を開けると、焼肉がジュージューと音を立て、笑い声と**会話が響**く世界。友人たちが集い、家族が祝い、見知らぬ者同士が焼き肉の喜びを分かち合って知り合う場所であった。ある夏の夜、若い女性カオリは、焼肉**店から**漂う魅惑的な香りに惹かれていた。好奇心旺盛な彼女は、店内に足を踏み入れると、すぐに活気ある雰囲気に包まれた。鉄板の上で肉が焼ける音、グラスの音が響き渡り、**期待に満ちた**シンフォニーを奏でている。

香織は焼き網が置かれたテーブルに座り、焼肉の冒険に出発した。霜降りの牛肉、**ジューシーな**豚肉、柔らかな鶏肉の盛り合わせが運ばれてくると、香織は期待に胸を膨らませた。霜降りの牛肉、ジューシーな豚肉、柔らかな鶏肉の盛り合わせが運ばれてくると、香織は期待に胸を膨らませ、肉を慎重に鉄板に並べ、ジュージューという音と立ち上る香ばしい煙に目を奪われる。一口食べると、香織の舌の上で様々な風味が踊る。**柔らかい牛肉は**バターのようにとろけ、濃厚で香ばしいエッセンスを放つ。豚肉はほのかな甘みがあり、鶏肉はスモーキーでジューシーな味わい。一粒一粒に感動を覚え、食の世界へ誘われる。しかし、焼肉は単に食べるだけでなく、共同**体験でも**あった。隣のテーブルの人たちと会話を交わしながら、おいしいごちそうに舌鼓を打つ。日本の伝統的な焼肉への愛情を共有することで、見知らぬ人たちが友達になったのです。

夜が更けるにつれて、香織のテーブルは**仲間意識に満ち**

savory essence. The pork carried a delicate sweetness, while the chicken delighted with its smoky and succulent taste. Each morsel was a revelation, a sensory **delight** that transported her to a world of culinary bliss. But yakiniku was not merely about the food; it was a communal **experience**. Kaori found herself engaged in conversation with the diners at neighboring tables, sharing stories and laughter as they savored the delectable feast before them. Strangers became friends, bound by their shared love for this traditional Japanese grilling tradition.

As the night wore on, Kaori's table became a vibrant hub of **camaraderie**. The tantalizing aroma of grilled meat mingled with the warmth of genuine connections. The yakiniku restaurant became a **sanctuary** of shared experiences and cherished memories. As Kaori bid farewell to her newfound friends and stepped back onto the bustling city streets, she carried with her a sense of fulfillment and **contentment**. Yakiniku had not only satisfied her hunger but had nourished her soul. It had reminded her of the simple joys of gathering around a table, celebrating life's pleasures, and savoring every moment. From that day forward, whenever Kaori craved a taste of connection and the **delight** of sizzling meat, she knew the yakiniku restaurant would be her sanctuary.

た活気ある空間となった。焼き肉の香りが漂い、人と人とのつながりが感じられる。焼肉屋は、共通の体験と大切な思い出が詰まった**聖域となった**。新しい仲間に別れを告げ、賑やかな街並みに戻った香織は、充実感と**満足感に包まれた**。焼肉は空腹を満たすだけでなく、心に栄養を与えてくれた。食卓を囲み、喜びを分かち合い、一瞬一瞬を味わうというシンプルな喜びを思い出させてくれたのである。その日以来、香織は、人とのつながりや肉のうまみを味わいたいとき、焼肉屋が自分の聖地になることを知った。

Comprehension Questions

1. What type of restaurant is described in the text?

2. What atmosphere greeted Kaori when she entered the yakiniku restaurant?

3. What types of meat were brought to Kaori's table?

4. How did Kaori feel as she placed the pieces of meat on the grill?

5. How would you describe the flavors Kaori experienced while eating the yakiniku?

6. Besides the food, what made the yakiniku experience special for Kaori?

7. How did Kaori engage with the diners at neighboring tables?

8. What transformed Kaori's table into a vibrant hub of camaraderie?

9. What did the yakiniku restaurant become for Kaori and others?

10. How did Kaori feel after her experience at the yakiniku restaurant?

理解度チェック問題

1. 本文中では、どのようなレストランが紹介されているのでしょうか。
2. 焼肉屋に入った香織は、どんな雰囲気で迎えてくれたのだろう。
3. 香織さんの食卓に運ばれてきたのは、どんなお肉だったのでしょうか。
4. 香織はどんな気持ちで肉をグリルに乗せたのだろう。
5. 焼肉を食べながら香織さんが感じた味を、どのように表現しますか?
6. 料理のほかに、カオリさんにとって焼肉体験が特別なものだったとは?
7. 香織は隣のテーブルのお客さんとどのように関わっていたのでしょうか。
8. 香織の食卓を仲間意識の強い活気ある拠点に変えたものは何か?
9. 焼肉屋は、香織さんたちにとってどんな存在になったのでしょうか。
10. 焼肉店での体験を経て、香織さんはどのように感じたのでしょうか。

Beppu Hot Springs

In the charming town of Beppu, nestled amidst rolling hills and surrounded by **lush** greenery, there existed a hidden gem—a collection of magnificent hot springs that painted the **landscape** with vibrant hues. From a young age, Hiro had been fascinated by the allure of these natural wonders. The tales of soothing waters and mystical healing powers ignited a sense of **adventure** within him. One sunny morning, Hiro set out to explore the renowned Beppu Hot Springs. As he ventured deeper into the town, a symphony of bubbling water and steam enveloped him. The air was thick with a **delicate** mist, creating an ethereal atmosphere. Hiro's eyes widened with excitement as he discovered the diverse array of hot springs scattered throughout the area.

His first stop was the iconic "Hells of Beppu." These were not traditional hot springs for bathing, but rather stunning natural **geothermal** sites, each with its own unique character. Hiro marveled at the vibrant reds and blues of the "Blood Pond Hell," caused by minerals present in the water. He then witnessed the geyser-like eruptions of steam from the "Tornado Hell." The "Sea Hell" **captivated** him with its mesmerizing cobalt blue waters, while the "White Pond Hell" stood out with

別府温泉

緑豊かな丘陵地帯に囲まれた別府の町には、鮮やかな色彩を放つ温泉がありました。ヒロは、幼い頃からその魅力に取り憑かれていた。そして、その温泉の魅力に惹かれ、**冒険心**を掻き立てられた。ある晴れた日の朝、ヒロは別府温泉の探索に出かけた。別府温泉の奥に進むと、湯けむりと水のハーモニーに包まれる。空気は霧に包まれ、幽玄な雰囲気に包まれている。別府には、さまざまな温泉が点在している。

最初に訪れたのは、別府を象徴する "別府の地獄 "だった。これらは入浴用の伝統的な温泉ではなく、自然の**地熱を利用した**素晴らしい場所であり、それぞれがユニークな個性をもっていました。血の池地獄」では、水に含まれる鉱物の影響で、赤や青の鮮やかな色彩に驚嘆した。そして、「竜巻地獄」では間欠泉のように蒸気が噴出する様子を目の当たりにした。コバルトブルーの海が**魅力の** "海地獄"、乳白色の "白池地獄"。どの場所も、自然の力強さと美しさを感じられる場所だった。そんな**中**、ヒロは温泉の露天風呂に足を運んだ。ミネラル豊富なお湯が体を包み込み、旅の疲れや緊張をほぐしてくれる。湯船につかりながら、風光明媚な景色を眺め、地球のエネルギーとの深いつながりを感じた。

別府温泉を巡るヒロの旅は、森の中に佇む素朴な秘湯から、パノラマビューが楽しめるモダンな豪華**施設**まで、**さまざまな**温泉を巡る。それぞれの温泉が独自の雰囲気を持ち、訪れる人にユニークな体験を提供していた。ヒロは、このような不思議な温泉で、静けさと静けさに包まれるのを楽しんでいた。太陽が沈み始め、**水平線が黄**

its milky white hue. Each site was a testament to the power and beauty of nature. Eager to experience the soothing waters **firsthand**, Hiro made his way to one of the open-air hot spring baths. The warm, mineral-rich waters enveloped his body, melting away the **fatigue** and tension of his journey. As he soaked, he gazed out at the picturesque landscape, feeling a profound connection to the earth's energy.

Hiro's journey through the Beppu Hot Springs continued as he explored **various** onsens, ranging from rustic, secluded baths nestled in the forest to modern, luxurious **establishments** with panoramic views. Each hot spring had its own ambiance, offering a unique experience for visitors. Hiro relished the tranquility and serenity that enveloped him in these magical oases. As the sun began to set, casting a golden glow over the **horizon**, Hiro reflected on his adventure. The Beppu Hot Springs had exceeded his expectations, not only in their natural beauty but also in the sense of rejuvenation and spiritual renewal they offered. He realized that these hot springs were not merely places to bathe; they were sanctuaries for the body, mind, and **soul**.

金色に輝く中、ヒロは自分の冒険を振り返った。別府温泉は、その自然の美しさだけでなく、若返りや精神的な回復をもたらすという意味でも、期待以上のものだった。この温泉は、単に入浴する場所ではなく、身体と心、そして**魂**のための聖域なのだ、と彼は悟った。

Comprehension Questions

1. What ignited Hiro's sense of adventure and fascination with the Beppu Hot Springs?

2. How would you describe the atmosphere in Beppu as Hiro explored the hot springs?

3. What were the "Hells of Beppu," and what made them unique compared to traditional hot springs?

4. Describe the colors and characteristics of the different hot springs Hiro encountered in the "Hells of Beppu."

5. Why did Hiro choose to visit one of the open-air hot spring baths?

6. How did Hiro feel as he soaked in the warm, mineral-rich waters?

7. What were the different types of onsens Hiro explored, and how did they vary?

8. How did Hiro feel about the tranquility and serenity he experienced in the hot springs?

9. What did Hiro realize about the Beppu Hot Springs in terms of their offerings beyond physical beauty?

10. How would you describe the overall impact of the Beppu Hot Springs on Hiro's body, mind, and soul?

理解度チェック問題

1. ヒロさんの冒険心に火をつけ、別府温泉の魅力に取り憑かれた理由とは?
2. ヒロが温泉を探検した別府の雰囲気はどうでしたか?
3. 別府の地獄」とは何だったのか、従来の温泉と比較して何が特徴的だったのか。
4. "別府の地獄"でヒロが出会ったさまざまな温泉の色や特徴を説明する。
5. ヒロはなぜ、ある温泉の露天風呂を選んだのでしょうか?
6. ミネラルたっぷりの温かいお湯に浸かったヒロは、どんな気持ちだったのでしょうか。
7. ヒロが探求したオンセンは、どのような種類で、どのように変化したのでしょうか?
8. 温泉で体験した静けさや穏やかさを、ヒロはどのように感じていたのでしょうか。
9. 別府温泉が持つ、肉体的な美しさ以外の魅力に、ヒロは何を感じたのでしょうか。
10. 別府温泉がヒロの身体、心、魂に与えた全体的な影響をどのように説明しますか?

The Genpei War

In the era of feudal Japan, a time marked by samurai valor and clan rivalries, the nation found itself engulfed in the **flames** of the Genpei War. It was a conflict that pitted the powerful Taira clan against the resolute Minamoto clan, both vying for control over the imperial throne. Amidst the chaos and **bloodshed**, a young warrior named Takeshi found himself swept into the tide of history. Takeshi hailed from a humble village, where tales of honor and bravery echoed through the winds. Inspired by the heroic deeds of the samurai, he dedicated his life to the pursuit of martial prowess. With unwavering **determination**, Takeshi honed his skills with the sword, longing for an opportunity to prove his worth on the battlefield. His moment arrived when he joined the ranks of Minamoto no Yoshitsune, a brilliant general leading the Minamoto forces. Clad in armor and armed with his katana, Takeshi marched alongside his **comrades**, a mix of seasoned veterans and eager warriors like himself. The horrors of war were starkly different from the romanticized tales Takeshi had heard, but he steeled his resolve, ready to face the perils that lay ahead.

The battles that followed were intense and brutal, the clash of **steel** and the screams of the fallen filling the air. Takeshi fought

源平合戦

武士の武勇と藩の対立に彩られた封建時代の日本が、源平合戦の**炎に包まれた**。平家と源氏が皇位継承をめぐって争ったのである。**そんな中**、一人の若い武士が歴史の流れに巻き込まれていく。タケシは、名誉や勇気の物語が風に乗って響く、質素な村の出身でした。武志は、侍の英雄的な行為に触発され、武勇の追求に人生を捧げました。戦場で自分の価値を証明する機会を待ち望みながら、揺るぎない**決意**で剣の腕を磨いた。その時、源義経の軍門に下ることになる。鎧に身を包み、刀で武装したタケシは、熟練したベテランと熱心な戦士が混在する**仲間たち**と共に行進した。戦の悲惨さは、武が聞いていたロマンチックな話とは全く違っていたが、彼は覚悟を決めて、目の前の危険に立ち向かう覚悟を決めた。

その後に続く戦いは激しく残酷で、**鋼鉄の衝突**と倒れた人の悲鳴が空気を満たしました。タケシは不屈の勇気で戦い、仲間を守り、一族の名誉を守りたいという**思い**で心を燃やした。刀を振るうたびに敵陣を切り裂き、その決意は決して**揺らぐことはなかった**。戦争が進むにつれ、タケシは紛争がもたらす悲惨な結果を目の当たりにしました。村が灰になり、家族がバラバラになり、**権力の追求**のために命が奪われるのを目の当たりにした。責任の重さに耐えかねて、武は戦争の真の目的を問うようになる。

壇ノ浦の決戦では、源氏の軍勢と平氏の軍勢が激突した。海は血で赤く染まり、船は炎に包まれ、戦士たちは**生き残る**ために必死で戦った。武志の前に立ちはだかったのは、卓越した技量と覚悟を持つ相手だった。両者の

with unyielding courage, his heart burning with the **desire** to protect his comrades and bring honor to his clan. With each swing of his blade, he carved a path through enemy lines, his determination never **faltering**. As the war unfolded, Takeshi witnessed firsthand the devastating consequences of conflict. He saw villages reduced to ashes, families torn apart, and lives lost in the pursuit of **power**. The weight of responsibility pressed upon him, and he questioned the true purpose of war.

In a decisive battle at Dan-no-ura, the Minamoto forces clashed with the Taira fleet. The waters ran red with blood as ships were **engulfed** in flames and warriors fought desperately for **survival**. Takeshi found himself facing an opponent of great skill and resolve. Their blades clashed, the sound reverberating through the chaos of the battlefield. In a moment of intense focus, Takeshi landed a decisive blow, felling his adversary and turning the tide of the battle in favor of the Minamoto clan. With victory **achieved**, Takeshi stood among his victorious comrades. As he surveyed the aftermath of the war, he felt a mix of emotions. The Genpei War had been a **crucible** that tested his mettle and reshaped his perspective. It had taught him the true cost of conflict and the importance of peace.

刃がぶつかり合い、その音は戦場の混乱に響いた。武は一瞬のうちに決定的な一撃を放ち、敵を倒し、戦いの流れを源氏に有利にした。勝利を**収めた武は**、勝利した仲間たちの中に立ちました。戦況を見渡しながら、武はさまざまな感慨を抱いた。源平合戦は、自分の度量が試され、考え方が変わる**坩堝であった**。争いの代償と平和の大切さを教えてくれた。

Comprehension Questions

1. What historical period is the story set in?

2. Who were the main opposing clans in the Genpei War?

3. What inspired Takeshi to dedicate his life to martial prowess?

4. Who was the leader of the Minamoto forces?

5. How did Takeshi feel about the realities of war compared to the romanticized tales he had heard?

6. What were some of the consequences of the war that Takeshi witnessed?

7. Where did the decisive battle between the Minamoto and Taira forces take place?

8. How did Takeshi contribute to the Minamoto clan's victory in the battle?

9. How did Takeshi feel as he surveyed the aftermath of the war?

10. What lessons did Takeshi learn from his experiences in the Genpei War?

理解度チェック問題

1. 物語の舞台となるのは、どのような時代なのでしょうか?
2. 源平合戦で主に対立した一族は誰ですか?
3. 武が格闘技に人生を捧げるようになったきっかけは?
4. 源氏軍のリーダーは誰だったのでしょうか?
5. 武は戦争の現実を、ロマンチックに語られる物語と比較してどのように感じたのだろうか。
6. 武が目撃した戦争の結果には、どのようなものがあったのでしょうか。
7. 源氏と平氏の決戦はどこで行われたのでしょうか?
8. 武は源氏の戦勝にどのように貢献したのでしょうか。
9. 武はどのような気持ちで戦争の余波を調査していたのでしょうか。
10. 源平合戦の経験から、武はどのような教訓を得たのでしょうか。

Fushimi Inari Taisha

In the ancient city of Kyoto, nestled among the **vibrant** cherry blossom trees and serene temples, stood Fushimi Inari Taisha, a shrine renowned for its thousands of vermilion torii gates. The sun cast a warm glow upon the sacred grounds as visitors from around the world flocked to witness its **mystical** allure. Among the visitors was a young woman named Ayumi. She had heard tales of the shrine's ethereal beauty and the **spiritual** energy that permeated its pathways. With a sense of reverence and curiosity, Ayumi stepped through the towering entrance gate, feeling a surge of anticipation. The path before her was lined with **countless** vermilion torii gates, forming a mesmerizing tunnel that led deeper into the spiritual realm.

As Ayumi ventured forth, she felt a hushed stillness **enveloping** her. The air was filled with the soft whispers of prayers and the rustling of leaves. Each step she took brought her closer to the heart of the shrine, where the spirit of Inari, the Shinto deity of rice and **prosperity**, resided. Ayumi marveled at the intricate details adorning the torii gates, their vibrant color contrasting against the lush greenery. As she meandered through the winding paths, Ayumi encountered **statues** of foxes, the sacred messengers of Inari. These statues stood as guardians, their wise

伏見稲荷大社

桜の名所として知られる京都の伏見稲荷大社には、朱色の鳥居が何本も立っている。朱色の鳥居が何本も並ぶ伏見稲荷大社は、太陽の光に照らされ、**神秘的な雰囲気に包まれていた。**その中に、あゆみという名の若い女性がいた。彼女は、この神社の幽玄な美しさと、参道に漂う**霊的なエネルギーの話を聞いていた。**あゆみは、畏敬の念と好奇心を胸に、聳え立つ門をくぐり、期待に胸を膨らませていた。目の前には、朱色の鳥居が**無数に並び、霊界の奥へと続く**魅惑的なトンネルが広がっていた。

あゆみが歩き出すと、静寂に**包まれるのを感じた。**祈りの声と葉のざわめきに包まれた空気。歩を進めるごとに、稲荷の神霊が宿る神社の中心部に近づいていく。鳥居に施された緻密な細工に驚嘆し、その鮮やかな色彩が豊かな緑と対照的であることに目を見張った。曲がりくねった道を歩いていると、稲荷の神使であるキツネの**像に出会う。**この狐の像が守護神として立ちはだかり、その賢明な眼差しが行き交う人々を観察している。あゆみは、この神秘的な生き物とのつながりを感じ、彼らの**存在が**自分の旅を導いてくれていることを感じた。

丘の頂上で、あゆみは神社の本殿にたどり着いた。そして、深い畏敬の念と感謝の念を込めて頭を下げ、祈りの言葉を捧げた。その神聖な空間で、彼女は深い安らぎと**神との一体感を感じた。**そして、その祈りの声が心に響き、新たな目的意識と希望で心が満たされた。**山頂から**下りたあゆみは、山腹に広がる広大な鳥居のネットワークを探索しつづけた。鳥居のひとつひとつは、個人や企業による寄付を示すもので、稲荷への奉納を象徴してい

eyes observing all who passed by. Ayumi sensed a connection with these mystical creatures, feeling their **presence** guiding her journey.

At the summit of the hill, Ayumi reached the main hall of the shrine. She offered her prayers, bowing in deep reverence and gratitude. In that sacred space, she felt a profound sense of peace and unity with the **divine**. The echoes of her prayers resonated within her, filling her heart with a renewed sense of purpose and hope. Descending from the **summit**, Ayumi continued to explore the vast network of torii gates that stretched across the mountainside. Each gate marked a donation by individuals or businesses, a symbolic act of devotion to Inari. Ayumi paused at one particularly striking gate, the sunlight filtering through its lattice **pattern**. In that moment, she understood the beauty of collective faith and the power of unity in creating a sacred space. As Ayumi bid farewell to Fushimi Inari Taisha, she carried within her a sense of awe and **serenity**. The experience had left an indelible mark on her spirit, igniting a deeper connection with the divine and a newfound appreciation for the harmonious blend of nature and spirituality.

る。あゆみは、特に印象的な鳥居の前で立ち止まり、その格子**模様に**陽の光が差し込むのを見た。その瞬間、彼女は集団信仰の美しさと、神聖な空間を作り上げる団結の力を理解した。伏見稲荷大社に別れを告げるとき、彼女は畏怖と**静寂の感覚を胸に抱いた**。この体験は、彼女の精神に忘れがたい足跡を残し、神との深いつながりと、自然とスピリチュアリティの調和に対する新たな感謝の念を呼び起こしたのです。

Comprehension Questions

1. Where is Fushimi Inari Taisha located?

2. What is Fushimi Inari Taisha renowned for?

3. What was Ayumi's motivation for visiting Fushimi Inari Taisha?

4. Describe the atmosphere Ayumi encountered as she ventured deeper into the shrine.

5. What is the significance of the torii gates at Fushimi Inari Taisha?

6. What role do the fox statues play in the shrine?

7. What did Ayumi feel when she reached the main hall of the shrine?

8. How did Ayumi perceive the network of torii gates across the mountainside?

9. What symbolic act do the gates represent?

10. How did Ayumi's experience at Fushimi Inari Taisha impact her?

理解度チェック問題

1. 伏見稲荷大社はどこにあるのですか?
2. 伏見稲荷大社は何で有名なんですか?
3. あゆみさんが伏見稲荷大社を訪れた動機は何だったのでしょうか。
4. あゆみが神社の奥に進んでいったときに出会った雰囲気を描写してください。
5. 伏見稲荷大社の鳥居にはどのような意味があるのでしょうか?
6. 狐の像は、神社の中でどのような役割を担っているのでしょうか。
7. 本殿にたどり着いたあゆみさんは、どんなことを感じたのでしょうか。
8. 山肌に張り巡らされた鳥居のネットワークを、あゆみはどう受け止めたのだろうか。
9. ゲートはどのような象徴的な行為を表しているのでしょうか?
10. 伏見稲荷大社での体験は、あゆみさんにどのような影響を与えたのでしょうか。

Haruki Murakami

Haruki Murakami sat at his desk, surrounded by piles of books and stacks of handwritten notes. The room was filled with an air of quiet **contemplation** as he prepared to embark on his next literary journey. The world knew him as a renowned author, a master of blending reality and fantasy in his novels. But behind the **enigmatic** smile and the piercing gaze of his eyes, Murakami carried a depth of thoughts and emotions that few could fathom. As he began to write, Murakami found himself transported to a realm where dreams and **memories** intertwined. Characters materialized before him, their voices echoing through the corridors of his mind. They whispered their stories, fragments of their lives that yearned to be told. Murakami meticulously crafted their **narratives**, allowing their hopes, fears, and desires to unfold on the pages of his manuscript.

In his storytelling, Murakami wove intricate tapestries of emotions and **philosophies**. He explored the existential questions that haunted his own consciousness—the nature of identity, the meaning of love, and the delicate balance between reality and illusion. Each word he penned held a piece of his soul, a **reflection** of his own inner journey. The process

村上春樹

村上春樹は、山積みの本と手書きのメモの束に囲まれながら、机に向かっていた。部屋は静かな**思索の空気に包まれ**、彼は次の文学の旅に出る準備をしていた。現実とファンタジーを融合させた小説の名手として、世間は彼を有名な作家として知っていた。しかし、**謎めいた微笑み**と鋭い眼差しの奥には、誰も理解できないような深い思考と感情を秘めていた。村上は、書き始めると、夢と**記憶が**交錯する世界へと誘われるのを感じた。キャラクターが目の前に現れ、その声が心の廊下に響く。彼らは、語り継がれることを切望している人生の断片を囁いた。村上は、彼らの**物語を**丹念に作り上げ、彼らの希望、恐怖、欲望を原稿用紙の上に展開させた。

村上春樹は、そのストーリーテリングにおいて、感情や**哲学の**複雑なタペストリーを織り成しました。アイデンティティーの本質、愛の意味、現実と幻想の微妙なバランスなど、自らの意識につきまとう実存的な問いを探求したのである。彼が書く言葉のひとつひとつは、彼の魂のかけらであり、彼自身の内なる旅路を**映し出すものだった**。その過程は、必ずしも容易なものではなかった。村上は、自分の創作物の**価値を疑うような**、頭の中のしつこい声に悩まされることがあった。しかし、彼は自分の想像力と読者の支持から力を得て、忍耐強く努力した。自分の言葉には、人の心を動かし、感情を揺さぶり、**文学の**世界に没頭する人の不思議な感覚に火をつける力があることを、彼は知っていた。

村上春樹の物語が形づくられるにつれ、彼は自らの宇宙の**設計者で**あると同時に探検家でもあるようになった。

was not always easy. Murakami faced moments of self-doubt, the nagging voice in his head questioning the **worthiness** of his creations. But he persevered, drawing strength from the power of his imagination and the support of his loyal readers. He knew that his words had the ability to touch lives, to stir emotions, and to ignite a sense of wonder in those who immersed themselves in his **literary** world.

As Murakami's stories took shape, he became both the **architect** and the explorer of his own universe. He delved into the depths of his characters' psyches, peeling back the layers of their **consciousness** to expose the raw essence of their being. In his writing, he sought to capture the beauty of the ordinary, to find meaning in the mundane, and to embrace the enigmatic nature of existence. Hours turned into days, and days into weeks as Murakami continued his solitary quest. The outside world faded away, and his words became his refuge, his sanctuary. With each completed novel, he emerged from his creative cocoon, offering his work to the eager readers who awaited his next **masterpiece**. Haruki Murakami understood that storytelling was an art form that transcended boundaries. Through his novels, he bridged the gap between cultures, inviting readers from all corners of the globe to delve into the enigmatic **landscapes** of his imagination.

彼は登場人物の深層心理に分け入り、**意識の層**をはがし、その生の本質をあぶり出す。そして、平凡なものの中に意味を見いだし、存在の謎めいた性質を受け入れようとしたのです。村上は孤独な探求を続けながら、時間は日になり、日になり、週になった。外界は消え去り、言葉は彼の避難所となり、聖域となった。小説が完成するたびに、彼は創作の繭から抜け出し、次の**傑作を待ち望む**熱心な読者たちに作品を提供した。村上春樹は、ストーリーテリングが境界を超えた芸術であることを理解していた。彼は小説を通して、文化間のギャップを埋め、世界中の読者を彼の想像の中の謎めいた**風景に**誘ったのです。

Comprehension Questions

1. What surrounded Haruki Murakami as he sat at his desk?

2. How is Haruki Murakami known in the world of literature?

3. What happens to Murakami as he begins to write?

4. How does Murakami describe the characters that materialize before him?

5. What does Murakami explore in his storytelling?

6. What challenges does Murakami face during the writing process?

7. What does Murakami draw strength from?

8. How does Murakami view the power of his words?

9. How does Murakami approach his characters' psyches in his writing?

10. What does Murakami believe about storytelling and its impact on readers?

理解度チェック問題

1. 机に向かう村上春樹を取り囲んでいたものは何だったのか。
2. 村上春樹は、文学の世界ではどのように知られているのでしょうか?
3. 書き始めた村上はどうなるのか?
4. 村上は、目の前に実体化したキャラクターをどのように表現しているのだろうか。
5. 村上はストーリーテリングの中で何を探求しているのだろうか。
6. 村上さんが執筆中に直面した課題とは?
7. 村上さんは何から力を得ているのでしょうか。
8. 村上は自分の言葉の力をどう捉えているのだろうか。
9. 村上さんは、登場人物の心理にどのようにアプローチして文章を書いているのでしょうか。
10. 村上は、ストーリーテリングとそれが読者に与える影響について、どのように考えているのだろうか。

Nikujaga

In a quaint Japanese kitchen, the aroma of **simmering** ingredients filled the air. Mitsuki, a young chef with a passion for traditional cuisine, stood over the stove, preparing a beloved dish known as Nikujaga. The dish was a medley of tender beef, potatoes, **carrots**, and onions cooked in a savory soy-based broth. Mitsuki had learned the recipe from her grandmother, who had passed down the family tradition with great pride. As Mitsuki stirred the pot, **memories** of her childhood flooded her mind. She recalled the comforting scent of Nikujaga that would waft through their home, drawing the family together at the dinner table. It was a dish that symbolized warmth and **togetherness**, a culinary embrace that nourished both body and soul.

With each ingredient carefully measured and added, Mitsuki poured her love and memories into the pot. The simmering broth transformed the raw **ingredients** into a harmonious symphony of flavors, carrying the essence of tradition and heritage. Mitsuki knew that Nikujaga was more than just a dish—it was a connection to her roots, a **reminder** of the generations before her who had found solace in its simple yet profound taste. As the dish cooked, Mitsuki's **anticipation**

ニクジャガ

古風な日本の厨房では、食材を**煮込む**香りが充満している。伝統的な料理に情熱を注ぐ若きシェフ、ミツキがコンロに向かい、「ニクジャガ」と呼ばれる愛すべき料理を作っていた。牛肉、ジャガイモ、**ニンジン**、タマネギを醤油ベースのスープで煮込んだ料理である。ミツキは、祖母からレシピを教わり、誇りを持ってこの家の伝統を受け継いできた。鍋をかき混ぜていると、幼い頃の**記憶がよみがえってくる。**ニクジャガの心地よい香りが家中に漂い、家族が食卓を囲んでいたことを思い出した。それは、温かさと**一体感を象徴する**料理であり、心身ともに滋養を与えてくれる料理であった。

食材をひとつひとつ丁寧に計量して加えながら、美月は鍋に愛と思い出を注いでいった。煮えたぎるスープが、**食材の味を**調和させ、伝統と継承のエッセンスを運びます。ニクジャガは単なる料理ではなく、自分のルーツとのつながりであり、シンプルで奥深い味わいに安らぎを見出した先人たちの**思い出でもあるのだ、と美津紀**は知っていた。料理が出来上がるにつれ、ミツキは**期待に胸を膨らませた。**鍋から香ばしい湯気が立ち上り、五感を刺激して、自分の努力の結晶を味わうように誘う。そして、いよいよニクジャガをお椀に盛り付けると、スプーン1本1本が色と質感の**モザイクのようだった。**そして、家族で食卓を囲み、目を輝かせながら食べる。一口食べると、舌の上で味覚が踊り、満足そうな**声が上がる。**

柔らかい牛肉は口の中でとろけ、ジャガイモとニンジンは香ばしいスープを吸い込んだ。まさに至福のひとときであり、食が人と人を結びつける魔法を**証明するもので**

grew. The fragrant steam rose from the pot, teasing her senses and beckoning her to savor the culmination of her efforts. Finally, she ladled the Nikujaga into bowls, each spoonful a **mosaic** of colors and textures. Mitsuki invited her family to gather around the table, their eyes lighting up with excitement. The first bite brought a **chorus** of satisfied murmurs, as the flavors danced on their tongues.

The tender beef melted in their mouths, while the potatoes and carrots soaked up the savory broth. It was a moment of pure bliss, a **testament** to the magic that happens when food brings people together. As they savored the Nikujaga, laughter filled the room, blending with the clinking of **chopsticks** and the contented sighs of a shared meal. Mitsuki looked around at her loved ones, their smiles reflecting the joy she had infused into the dish. Nikujaga had not only **nourished** their bodies but had also nourished their bonds, strengthening the ties that bound them. In that kitchen, Mitsuki realized the power of food to **transcend** time and distance, to bridge generations and create lasting memories. With each bite of Nikujaga, she vowed to carry on the tradition, passing down the recipe and the love it contained to future generations.

あった。ニクジャガを味わっている間、部屋には笑い声があふれ、**箸**の音や食事の満足げなため息が混じった。ミツキは、愛する人たちを見渡した。その笑顔は、彼女が料理に込めた喜びを反映していた。ニクジャガは、彼らの体だけでなく、絆を育み、絆を深めていた。この時、美津紀は、食が時間や距離を超え、世代を超え、思い出を作る力を持つことを実感した。ニクジャガを食べるたびに、彼女は伝統を受け継ぎ、レシピとそれに込められた愛情を後世に伝えていこうと誓った。

Comprehension
Questions

1. What dish is Mitsuki preparing in the Japanese kitchen?

2. What are the main ingredients of Nikujaga?

3. Who did Mitsuki learn the Nikujaga recipe from?

4. How does Mitsuki describe the scent of Nikujaga from her childhood?

5. What does Nikujaga symbolize to Mitsuki?

6. What does Mitsuki pour into the pot as she cooks Nikujaga?

7. How does Mitsuki describe the transformation of the ingredients in the pot?

8. What emotions does Mitsuki experience as the dish cooks?

9. How does Mitsuki's family react when she serves the Nikujaga?

10. What realization does Mitsuki have about the power of food in the kitchen?

理解度チェック問題

1. 日本のキッチンでミツキが作っている料理は何でしょう?

2. ニクジャガの主な成分は何ですか?

3. ミツキは誰からニクジャガのレシピを学んだのでしょうか?

4. ミツキは、幼少期のニクジャガの香りをどのように表現しているのでしょうか。

5. ニクジャガは、ミツキにとって何を象徴しているのでしょうか。

6. ニクジャガを調理するミツキは、鍋に何を注ぐのでしょうか?

7. ミツキは、鍋の中の食材が変化していく様子をどのように表現しているのでしょうか。

8. 料理が出来上がるまでの間、ミツキはどんな感情を抱くのでしょうか。

9. ミツキがニクジャガに仕えるとき、ミツキの家族はどのような反応をするのでしょうか。

10. キッチンの食の力について、ミツキはどんな気づきを得たのでしょうか。

Odaiba

As the sun began its descent, casting a warm golden hue across Tokyo Bay, a young couple strolled hand in hand along the shores of Odaiba. The man, Hiroshi, and his **girlfriend**, Aiko, had chosen this iconic waterfront destination for a romantic evening. Odaiba, known for its futuristic **architecture** and vibrant atmosphere, provided the perfect backdrop for their special outing. Hiroshi and Aiko had met years ago in a bustling Tokyo café, their connection instantaneous. They shared a love for adventure and **exploration**, always seeking new experiences together. Tonight, their destination was the famous Rainbow Bridge, a breathtaking **structure** that spanned the bay, linking Odaiba to the heart of Tokyo. As they walked, the city's dazzling lights mirrored in the tranquil waters, creating a magical reflection.

Reaching the foot of the bridge, Hiroshi suggested they take a ride on the **futuristic** Yurikamome Line, an automated train that provided stunning views of the bay and the cityscape. Aiko's eyes sparkled with excitement as they boarded the sleek **carriage**. The train glided smoothly along the elevated tracks, offering panoramic vistas of Tokyo's skyline. As they arrived at their stop, Hiroshi and Aiko found themselves at the heart of

お台場

太陽が沈み始め、東京湾が暖かい黄金色に染まる頃、若いカップルがお台場の海岸を手をつないで歩いていた。男性・ヒロシとその**恋人**・アイコは、ロマンチックな夜を過ごすために、この象徴的なウォーターフロントの場所を選んだのだ。近未来的な**建築物**と活気に満ちた雰囲気で知られるお台場は、2人の特別なお出かけにぴったりの場所だったのです。ヒロシとアイコは数年前、東京の賑やかなカフェで出会い、すぐに心を通わせた。二人は冒険と**探検**が大好きで、いつも一緒に新しい経験を求めていました。今夜の目的地は、お台場と東京の中心を結ぶ、湾に架かる息を呑むような**建造物**、有名なレインボーブリッジだった。お台場と東京の中心部を結ぶこの橋は、湾内に架けられた息を呑むような建造物である。

橋のたもとで博は、湾や街並みが一望できる**近未来的な**自動運転列車「ゆりかもめ」に乗ることを提案した。愛子は目を輝かせながら、洗練された**車両に乗り込みました**。電車は高架をスムーズに走り、東京の街並みを一望することができる。駅に着くと、博と愛子はお台場の中心部にいた。賑やかなウォーターフロントは活気に満ちており、お二人はそのエネルギッシュな**雰囲気に包まれた**。お二人は、活気あふれるショッピングモールを巡り、おいしいスイーツに舌鼓を打ち、記念になるユニークなお土産を見つけました。愛子さまの笑い声が響く中、お二人はゲームセンターでゲームに挑戦したり、**クローマシン**での運試しに挑戦したりしました。

次に向かったのは、お台場のシンボルであり、喜びと**驚きの象徴である大観覧車**。観覧車に乗り込むと、目の前

Odaiba. The bustling waterfront was alive with activity, and the couple reveled in the energetic **atmosphere**. They explored the vibrant shopping malls, indulging in delectable treats and finding unique souvenirs to commemorate their visit. Aiko's laughter echoed through the air as they challenged each other to arcade games and tried their luck at a claw **machine**.

Their next stop was Odaiba's iconic Ferris wheel, a symbol of joy and **wonder**. As they ascended, the breathtaking view of the city unfolded before their eyes. Tokyo Tower, ablaze in vibrant lights, stood proudly in the distance, while the city's **skyscrapers** reached for the heavens. Aiko leaned her head on Hiroshi's shoulder, feeling the warmth of their connection in this elevated moment. The couple's final destination was a secluded waterfront park. They found a quiet spot **overlooking** the bay, surrounded by blooming cherry blossom trees. With a gentle breeze rustling through their hair, they sat together, reveling in the **serenity** of the moment. The sound of lapping waves and distant laughter created a symphony of tranquility. As they watched the lights of Tokyo dance across the water, Hiroshi took Aiko's hand in his and whispered, "This evening, this place, it's a testament to our love and the adventures we've shared. Odaiba will forever hold a special place in our hearts."

に広がるのは、息をのむような都会の絶景。遠くには、鮮やかな光に包まれた東京タワーが、そして天空には**高層ビル群がそびえ立っている**。愛子は博の肩に頭を預け、二人のつながりの温かさを感じながら、この高揚した時間を過ごしていました。二人が最後に向かったのは、人里離れた水辺の公園でした。湾を**見下ろす**静かな場所で、満開の桜の木に囲まれながら。髪を揺らすそよ風に吹かれながら、ふたりで**静かに時を過ごす**。波の音と笑い声が、静寂のシンフォニーを奏でます。東京の光が水面を舞うのを見ながら、ヒロシは愛子の手を握り、こうささやきました。「この夜、この場所は、私たちの愛と冒険の証しです。お台場は、私たちの心の中で永遠に特別な場所です"

Comprehension Questions

1. Where did Hiroshi and Aiko choose to spend their evening?

2. What is Odaiba known for?

3. How did Hiroshi and Aiko meet?

4. What is the famous structure that spans Tokyo Bay?

5. What type of train did Hiroshi suggest they ride?

6. What views did the Yurikamome Line offer?

7. What activities did Hiroshi and Aiko enjoy at the bustling waterfront?

8. What iconic landmark did they visit after the waterfront?

9. Describe the view from the Ferris wheel.

10. Where did Hiroshi and Aiko end their evening, and what was the atmosphere like there?

理解度チェック問題

1. ヒロシとアイコはどこで夜を過ごすことにしたのだろう。
2. お台場といえば?
3. ヒロシとアイコの出会いのきっかけは?
4. 東京湾に架かる有名な建造物は何ですか?
5. ヒロシはどんな列車に乗ることを提案したのだろう。
6. ゆりかもめ線はどんな景色を見せてくれたのでしょうか。
7. 賑やかなウォーターフロントで、ヒロシとアイコはどんなアクティビティを楽しんだのでしょうか。
8. ウォーターフロントの後に訪れた象徴的なランドマークとは?
9. 観覧車から見える景色を描写してください。
10. ヒロシとアイコはどこで夜を明かし、そこではどんな雰囲気があったのでしょうか。

The Painter's Muse

In the quaint town of Willowbrook, there lived a renowned painter named Julian. With his skilled brushstrokes and vivid **imagination**, Julian had earned a reputation as a master of his craft. Yet, his recent works lacked the spark of inspiration that once ignited his artistry. Desperate to rekindle his creative fire, Julian embarked on a journey to find his **muse**. One foggy morning, as Julian strolled through the mist-shrouded park, he spotted a young woman sitting on a bench. Her radiant smile and eyes gleaming with mystery captivated him. Julian approached her and introduced himself. Her name was Amelia. As Julian and Amelia conversed, a deep **connection** formed between them. She shared stories of her travels, of ancient civilizations and forgotten tales. Her words were like brushstrokes across Julian's imagination, creating **vibrant** scenes within his mind.

Inspired by their encounters, Julian invited Amelia to his studio. She marveled at the colorful chaos of his paintings adorning the walls. Julian explained his **creative** block and how he longed for a muse to guide him once more. Amelia, intrigued, offered herself as his muse. She became a living embodiment of inspiration, with each **interaction** sparking new artistic visions

絵描きのミューズ

ウィローブルックという古風な町に、ジュリアンという名の高名な画家が住んでいました。巧みな筆致と鮮やかな**想像力で**、**ジュリアンは**名画家として名を馳せていた。しかし、最近の彼の作品には、かつて彼の芸術性に火をつけたインスピレーションが欠けていた。創作の炎を再び燃やそうと、ジュリアンは**ミューズ探しの旅に出た**。ある霧の朝、霧に包まれた公園を散歩していたジュリアンは、ベンチに座っている若い女性を見つけた。その輝くような笑顔と神秘的な瞳に、ジュリアンは心を奪われた。ジュリアンは彼女に近づき、自己紹介をした。彼女の名前はアメリアといった。ジュリアンとアメリアは会話を交わすうちに、深い**絆で結ばれて**いった。彼女は旅の話、古代文明の話、忘れられた物語を話してくれた。彼女の言葉は、ジュリアンの想像力をかき立てる筆跡のようで、彼の心の中に**鮮やかな**情景を描き出した。

その出会いに触発されたジュリアンは、アメリアをアトリエに招き入れた。アメリアは、壁に飾られた色とりどりの絵に驚嘆する。ジュリアンは、**創作意欲がわかず、もう一度自分を導いてくれる**ミューズを渇望していることを説明する。アメリアは興味をそそられ、ミューズになることを申し出る。彼女はインスピレーションを体現する存在となり、**そのたびに**ジュリアンの中に新たな芸術的ヴィジョンが生まれました。彼女の**存在は**、彼の中に眠っていた情熱を呼び覚まし、彼の絵は再び命を吹き込まれた。そして、ジュリアンの芸術の発展とともに、2人の友情も深まっていった。アメリアの笑い声がスタジオに響き渡り、喜びと魔法で満たされた。ジュリアンは、アメリアだけでなく、彼女が開いてくれた**可能性の**

within Julian. Her **presence** awakened a dormant passion in him, and his paintings began to breathe with life once more. As Julian's art flourished, so did their friendship. Amelia's laughter echoed through the studio, filling it with joy and magic. Julian found himself falling in love, not only with Amelia but with the world of **possibilities** she opened for him.

But one day, Amelia vanished without a trace. Julian searched **frantically**, desperate to find his muse. His paintings, once vibrant and alive, grew dull and lifeless. Julian's heart ached for Amelia, and he feared he had lost her forever. Months passed, and Julian's paintings gathered dust in his **studio**. The world seemed colorless without Amelia's presence. Just as he was about to abandon hope, a gentle knock echoed through his studio door. It was Amelia, standing there with a sorrowful smile. She explained that she had been away, facing her own **demons** and rediscovering her own muse. Amelia had traveled to distant lands, seeking inspiration to bring back to Julian. With tears of joy, Julian embraced Amelia. He understood that her absence had been **necessary** for both their journeys. United once again, they ventured into new artistic realms, painting with renewed passion and purpose.

世界に恋をしている自分に気がついた。

しかし、ある日、アメリアは忽然と姿を消した。ジュリアンは、自分のミューズを見つけるために**必死**で探した。かつて生き生きとしていた彼の絵は、次第にくすんでいき、生気を失っていった。ジュリアンの心はアメリアを想い、永遠に失ってしまったのではないかと不安になった。月日は流れ、ジュリアンの絵は**アトリエ**で埃をかぶっていた。アメリアのいない世界は無色透明に見えた。希望を捨てようとしたとき、アトリエのドアを優しくノックする音が響いた。憂いを帯びた笑顔で立っているアメリアであった。彼女は、自分の悪魔と向き合い、自分のミューズを再発見するために、離れていたのだと説明した。アメリアは、ジュリアンのためにインスピレーションを求めて、遠い国まで旅をしてきたのだという。ジュリアンは喜びの涙を流しながら、アメリアを抱きしめた。二人の旅には、アメリアの不在が**必要だったのだと理解したのだ**。二人は再び結ばれ、新たな芸術の領域へと踏み出し、新たな情熱と目的を持って絵を描くようになった。

Comprehension Questions

1. What was Julian's profession?

2. Why did Julian embark on a journey?

3. What caught Julian's attention when he was strolling through the park?

4. How did Julian and Amelia connect with each other?

5. What did Amelia share with Julian during their conversations?

6. How did Julian's paintings change after Amelia became his muse?

7. What happened when Amelia disappeared?

8. How did Julian feel during Amelia's absence?

9. Where did Amelia go and what was she searching for?

10. How did Julian and Amelia's artistic journey continue after they reunited?

理解度チェック問題

1. ジュリアンの職業は何だったのか?

2. なぜジュリアンは旅に出たのか?

3. 公園を散歩していたジュリアンの目に留まったものは?

4. ジュリアンとアメリアは、どのように心を通わせたのでしょうか?

5. アメリアはジュリアンとの会話で何を話したのでしょうか?

6. アメリアがミューズになったことで、ジュリアンの絵はどのように変化したのでしょうか。

7. アメリアがいなくなった時、何が起こったのか?

8. アメリア不在の間、ジュリアンはどのように感じていたのでしょうか。

9. アメリアはどこへ行き、何を探していたのか。

10. ジュリアンとアメリアの芸術の旅は、再会後どのように続いていったのでしょうか。

A Brush with Destiny

In the sleepy town of Ashford, lived a young **artist** named Lily. With her vibrant imagination and deft brushstrokes, she possessed a unique talent that left spectators in awe. Her paintings seemed to come alive, telling stories of love, **adventure**, and the mysteries of the world. Yet, Lily felt a yearning deep within her soul. She longed for a chance encounter that would change the course of her artistic journey. One sunny morning, as Lily set up her easel in the park, she noticed a peculiar figure in the **distance**. It was an elderly man, dressed in a tattered coat, sitting alone on a bench. Something about him intrigued her, drawing her towards him like a moth to a flame. Tentatively, Lily approached the man and struck up a conversation. His name was Samuel, and he spoke of his lifelong love for art. Samuel shared tales of his own artistic endeavors and the countless **hurdles** he faced in pursuing his passion.

Inspired by Samuel's stories, Lily invited him to her studio. Samuel's eyes gleamed with **excitement** as he marveled at Lily's creations. He spoke of the beauty he saw in her work and the potential he sensed within her. Samuel became Lily's mentor, guiding her through the intricacies of **composition**,

運命の出会い

アシュフォードという静かな町に、リリーという名の若い**画家**が住んでいた。彼女の想像力と巧みな筆さばきは、見る者に畏敬の念を抱かせるほどユニークな才能を持っていました。彼女の絵はまるで生きているようで、愛や**冒険**、世界の謎を物語っている。しかし、リリーは心の奥底で切望を感じていた。彼女の芸術の旅路を変えるような偶然の出会いを待ち望んでいたのだ。ある晴れた日の朝、公園でイーゼルを立てていたリリーは、**遠くのほうに**奇妙な人影があるのに気づきました。ボロボロのコートを着た老人が、一人ベンチに座っているのだ。その姿に興味を持ったリリーは、まるで蛾が炎に吸い寄せられるように、彼のもとへ向かった。リリーは緊張しながらも、その男性に近づき、会話をした。彼はサミュエルと名乗り、芸術に対する生涯の愛情を語った。サミュエルは、自分の芸術活動や、情熱を追求するために直面した数え切れないほどの**困難の話をした。**

サミュエルの話に触発されたリリーは、彼をアトリエに招き入れた。サミュエルは目を輝かせ、リリーの作品に**感嘆の声を上げた。**サミュエルはリリーの作品に感動し、その美しさと可能性を語った。サミュエルはリリーの師匠となり、**構図**、色彩、感情の複雑さを指導していく。彼の指導のもと、リリーの作品はそれまでの枠を超え、開花していった。月日が経つにつれ、サミュエルの健康状態は悪化していった。リリーは、師匠の**活力**が失われていくのを悄然と見つめた。しかし、サミュエルはリリーの才能を信じ、揺るぎない意志を持っていた。最後の日、サミュエルはリリーに、使い古した小さなブラシを手渡した。そして、自分の大切な**宝物**であり、これ

color, and emotion. Under his tutelage, Lily's art blossomed, transcending the boundaries of her previous works. As months passed, Samuel's health began to decline. Lily watched with a heavy heart as her mentor's **vitality** faded. Yet, Samuel remained unwavering in his belief in Lily's talent. On his final day, Samuel handed Lily a small, worn-out brush. He told her it was his most cherished **possession** and that it was now time for her to carry on his legacy.

Devastated by Samuel's passing, Lily felt a surge of **determination**. She vowed to honor his memory by channeling his passion and wisdom through her art. With each stroke of the brush, Lily poured her emotions onto the canvas, breathing life into Samuel's teachings. Her paintings spoke of the **indomitable** spirit that had burned brightly in both Samuel and herself. Lily's art gained recognition, and her name became synonymous with brilliance. People marveled at the depth and richness of her work, unaware of the **humble** beginnings that had shaped her talent. Lily knew that Samuel's spirit guided her every stroke, forever entwined with her artistic journey. In the quiet of her studio, as Lily gazed at her masterpiece, she knew that her encounter with Samuel had been a brush with **destiny**.

からは自分がその遺志を継ぐ番であると告げた。

サミュエルの死後、リリーはある**決意を固めました**。サミュエルが残した情熱と知恵をアートで表現し、サミュエルの思い出を守ろうと。筆を走らせるたびに、リリーは自分の感情をキャンバスに注ぎ込み、サミュエルの教えに命を吹き込んでいった。リリーの絵は、サミュエルと自分自身の中にある**不屈の精神を表現していた**。リリーの絵は評判となり、彼女の名前は輝きの代名詞となった。人々は、彼女の才能を形成した**謙虚な出発点を知らないまま**、その作品の深さと豊かさに驚嘆した。リリーは、サミュエルの精神が彼女の一筆一筆を導き、彼女の芸術の旅路と永遠に結びついていることを知っていた。アトリエの静けさの中で、リリーは自分の傑作を見つめながら、サミュエルとの出会いが**運命の出会いであったことを知った**。

Comprehension Questions

1. Who is the protagonist of the story?

2. What is Lily's profession?

3. What is the initial feeling Lily experiences when she sees the elderly man on the bench?

4. What is the name of the elderly man Lily meets?

5. How does Samuel contribute to Lily's artistic growth?

6. What gift does Samuel give to Lily before he passes away?

7. How does Lily respond to Samuel's passing?

8. What does Lily vow to do after Samuel's death?

9. How do people react to Lily's artwork after she incorporates Samuel's teachings?

10. How does Lily perceive her encounter with Samuel in the end?

理解度チェック問題

1. 物語の主人公は誰なのか?

2. リリーさんの職業は?

3. リリーがベンチの老人を見たとき、最初に感じたことは何だろう。

4. リリーが出会った老人の名前は何でしょう?

5. サミュエルは、リリーの芸術的成長にどのように貢献しているのでしょうか?

6. サミュエルが亡くなる前に、リリーに贈ったプレゼントとは?

7. サミュエルの死去にリリーはどう対応するのか?

8. サミュエルの死後、リリーは何を誓うのか。

9. サミュエルの教えを取り入れたリリーの作品に、人々はどのような反応を示すのでしょうか。

10. リリーは最後にサミュエルとの出会いをどう受け止めているのだろうか。

Footsteps in the Sand

In a small coastal village, where the ocean kissed the shore,
there lived a young girl named Maya. With her **golden** hair
and sparkling blue eyes, Maya had an insatiable curiosity for
the world around her. She would spend hours exploring the
sandy beaches, collecting seashells and chasing **seagulls**. But
there was one thing that fascinated her more than anything
else—the mysterious footsteps that appeared on the sand every
morning. Each day, as the sun rose and painted the sky in hues
of orange and pink, Maya would rush to the beach to find the
freshly imprinted **footprints**. They were unlike any she had
ever seen before, delicate and ethereal, as if left by a creature
from another realm. Maya would follow the footsteps, tracing
their path along the shore, hoping they would lead her to the
enigmatic being behind them.

As years passed, Maya's fascination with the footsteps grew.
She would sketch them in her **notebook**, trying to capture
their elusive beauty. The village folk, intrigued by her obsession,
began to share their own **theories**. Some believed the footsteps
belonged to a mermaid, others to a mythical creature that
roamed the shores at night. But Maya remained determined
to uncover the truth. One stormy evening, as the wind howled

砂の上の足音

海辺の小さな村に、マヤという名の少女が住んでいました。**金色の髪と青い瞳を持つマヤ**は、周囲の世界に対して飽くなき好奇心を持っていました。砂浜で貝殻を集めたり、**カモメを追いかけたりして、何時間も過ごしていました**。毎朝、砂浜に現れる不思議な足音だ。太陽が昇り、空がオレンジとピンクに染まる頃、マヤはその**足跡を見つける**ために浜辺に駆けつけました。まるで別世界の生き物が残したかのような、繊細で幽玄な足跡だ。マヤはその足跡をたどり、海岸に沿った道をたどりながら、その背後にいる**謎めいた存在へと導いてくれることを願った。**

年月が経つにつれ、マヤは足音に魅了されるようになりました。マヤはその足跡を**ノート**に描き、そのとらえどころのない美しさを表現しようとしました。そんなマヤに興味を持った村人たちは、それぞれの**説を語り始めました**。ある人は人魚の足音、ある人は夜に海岸を徘徊する神話的な生物の足音だと考えた。しかし、マヤは真実を明らかにすることを決意しました。ある嵐の夜、風が吹き荒れ、波が岩に打ち付ける中、マヤは**遠く**でかすかな光が輝いていることに気づいた。浜辺の方だ。マヤは期待に胸を膨らませながら、その光を追いかけた。すると、水辺に若い女性が立っているのを発見した。銀色の髪が月明かりに照らされ、その瞳は**若さとは裏腹に聡明**である。

その女性は、海の秘密を守るセリーンと名乗った。マヤは、セリーンが謎の足音の主役であることに気づき、目を**見張った**。セリーンは、夜明けに海岸を歩き、海の美

and waves crashed against the rocks, Maya noticed a faint light shimmering in the **distance**. It was coming from the beach. She followed the glow, heart pounding with anticipation. To her astonishment, she discovered a young woman standing near the water's edge. She had silvery hair that glistened under the moonlight, and her eyes held a wisdom that belied her youthful **appearance**.

The woman introduced herself as Selene, the guardian of the ocean's secrets. Maya's eyes widened in **wonder** as she realized that Selene was the one responsible for the mysterious footsteps. Selene explained that she walked the shores at dawn, leaving her mark as a reminder of the **beauty** and power of the sea. She had observed Maya's unwavering curiosity and had chosen to reveal herself, sensing a kindred spirit in the young girl. Over time, Selene became Maya's mentor, teaching her about the ocean's wonders and the importance of preserving its fragile **ecosystem**. Maya's sketches transformed into breathtaking paintings, capturing the essence of the sea and the footprints that had first ignited her **imagination**. As Maya grew older, she took on the role of the village's guardian of the sea, passing on Selene's teachings to future generations.

しさと力を思い起こさせるために自分の足跡を残していると説明した。マヤの揺るぎない好奇心を見たセリーンは、マヤと心を通わせることができると思い、その姿を現したのです。やがてセリーンはマヤの師匠となり、海の不思議や壊れやすい**生態系を守ること**の大切さを教えてくれるようになりました。マヤのスケッチは、海のエッセンスと**想像力をかき立てた**足跡をとらえた、息をのむような絵画へと変化していきました。マヤは成長すると、村の海の守り神として、セリーンの教えを後世に伝えていくことになります。

Comprehension Questions

1. What fascinated Maya more than anything else in the coastal village?
2. Describe the footprints that Maya discovered on the beach each morning.
3. What did Maya hope to uncover by following the footsteps along the shore?
4. How did Maya express her fascination with the footprints?
5. What were some of the theories shared by the village folk about the origin of the footprints?
6. What did Maya notice one stormy evening that led her to the beach?
7. Describe Selene's appearance when Maya discovered her on the beach.
8. What did Selene reveal about her role in creating the mysterious footprints?
9. How did Maya's relationship with Selene evolve over time?
10. What role did Maya eventually take on in the village as a result of her encounters with Selene?

理解度チェック問題

1. 海岸沿いの村で、マヤを何よりも魅了したものは何だったのか。
2. マヤが毎朝浜辺で発見した足跡について説明する。
3. マヤは海岸の足跡をたどることで、何を発見しようとしたのだろう。
4. マヤは足跡の面白さをどう表現したのでしょうか。
5. 足跡の由来について、村の人たちが共有していた説にはどのようなものがあったのでしょうか。
6. ある嵐の夜、マヤは何に気づいて海辺に向かったのだろう。
7. マヤが海岸で発見したときのセレーネの姿を描写してください。
8. セリーンは、謎の足跡を作った自分の役割について、何を明かしたのでしょうか。
9. マヤとセリーンの関係は、時間の経過とともにどのように変化していったのでしょうか。
10. マヤはセレーネとの出会いをきっかけに、最終的に村の中でどんな役割を担うことになったのでしょうか。

Hidden Treasures

In the heart of a bustling city, amidst the towering **buildings** and crowded streets, there was an old bookstore called "Hidden Treasures." It was a place of magic, where books whispered tales of adventure and knowledge. The owner, Mr. Anderson, had spent his entire life collecting **rare** and forgotten books, carefully preserving them within the store's walls. However, the true allure of Hidden Treasures lay in its hidden secrets. One sunny afternoon, a young girl named Emily wandered into the bookstore. Her eyes widened in awe as she beheld the shelves lined with **books** of all shapes and sizes. Mr. Anderson greeted her with a warm smile, sensing the curiosity radiating from her. He invited her to explore and discover the **wonders** within the store's hidden corners.

As Emily meandered through the **labyrinthine** aisles, she noticed a peculiar bookshelf covered in a thin layer of dust. Intrigued, she carefully pushed aside the books, revealing a hidden **compartment**. Inside, she found a tattered leather-bound journal. Its pages were filled with handwritten notes and sketches, chronicling the adventures of past visitors who had stumbled upon Hidden Treasures' secrets. The journal spoke of a hidden doorway that led to a world beyond imagination.

隠された宝物

賑やかな街の中心、高くそびえるビルと混雑した通り
に、"秘宝"という古い書店がありました。そこは、本が
冒険と知識の物語をささやく、魔法のような場所だっ
た。店主のアンダーソン氏は、生涯をかけて珍しい本や
忘れ去られた本を集め、店内に大切に保存していた。し
かし、秘宝の本当の魅力は、その隠された秘密にありま
した。ある晴れた日の午後、エミリーという名の少女が
書店に迷い込んできた。大小さまざまな本が並ぶ棚に目
を見張り、感嘆の声を上げた。アンダーソン氏は、彼女
の好奇心を感じ取り、温かい笑顔で出迎えた。アンダー
ソン氏は、彼女の好奇心に応えて、店内のあちこちにあ
る不思議なものを探そうと誘った。

迷路のような通路を歩きながら、エミリーは薄い埃に覆
われた奇妙な本棚に目を留めた。興味津々で本を押しのの
けると、隠れた収納スペースが現れた。その中には、ボ
ロボロの革装の日記があった。手書きのメモやスケッチ
で埋め尽くされたページには、ヒドゥン・トレジャーズの
秘密を知った過去の訪問者の冒険が綴られていた。その
日記には、想像を絶する世界へと続く隠された扉につい
て書かれていた。そして、好奇心旺盛な人を宝物へと導
く手がかりと謎が記されていた。エミリーは、目の前に
広がるチャンスに胸を躍らせた。アンダーソン氏は、こ
の発見の喜びを語り、微笑みながら、「さあ、冒険の旅
に出よう」と励ました。

エミリーは日記を手に、謎を解き、手がかりを頼りに迷
路のような本の中を進んでいく。一見すると普通の本棚
を押すと、隠された通路が現れる。そこは、陽光が降り

It detailed clues and riddles that would guide the curious seeker to the **treasure** hidden within. Emily's heart raced with excitement as she realized the opportunity that lay before her. She shared her discovery with Mr. Anderson, who smiled knowingly, encouraging her to embark on her own **adventure**.

Armed with the **journal**, Emily deciphered the riddles and followed the clues through the maze of books. She pushed a seemingly ordinary bookshelf and revealed a concealed passage. It led her to a hidden garden, bathed in sunlight and filled with **enchanting** flora. The air was thick with the scent of flowers, and a gentle breeze whispered secrets in her ear. Emily explored the garden, following a winding path that led her to a magnificent oak tree. At its base, nestled within the earth, she discovered a small wooden box. Inside, she found a **collection** of ancient coins, sparkling gemstones, and a handwritten note. The note spoke of the true treasures in life—friendship, love, and the beauty of the world around us. Overwhelmed with **gratitude**, Emily returned to Hidden Treasures and shared her experience with Mr. Anderson. The two of them realized that the real magic of the bookstore was not in the hidden treasures, but in the stories and connections it forged.

注ぎ、**美しい**植物が咲き乱れる秘密の花園だった。花の香りが漂い、そよ風が秘密を囁いている。エミリーは庭を探索し、曲がりくねった道を進んでいくと、立派なオークの木にたどり着いた。その根元、土の中に小さな木箱を発見した。中には、古代のコインや宝石、そして手書きのメモが収められていた。そこには、友情、愛、そして世界の美しさという、人生の真の宝物が書かれていた。エミリーは**感謝**の気持ちでいっぱいになり、秘宝に戻り、アンダーソン氏にその体験を話した。2人は、書店の本当の魔法は、隠された宝物ではなく、書店が生み出す物語やつながりにあることを悟った。

Comprehension Questions

1. What is the name of the bookstore in the story?

2. What was the true allure of Hidden Treasures?

3. Who is the owner of the bookstore?

4. What did Emily discover when she pushed aside the books on the peculiar bookshelf?

5. What did the tattered leather-bound journal contain?

6. What did the journal speak of?

7. Where did the hidden passage in the bookstore lead Emily?

8. What did Emily find at the base of the magnificent oak tree?

9. What did the handwritten note inside the wooden box speak of?

10. What did Emily and Mr. Anderson realize about the real magic of the bookstore?

理解度チェック問題

1. 物語に登場する書店の名前は何でしょうか?
2. ヒドゥン・トレジャーの本当の魅力は何だったのか?
3. 書店の店主は誰なのでしょうか?
4. 特異な本棚の本を押しのけたエミリーは、何を発見したのだろうか。
5. ボロボロの革表紙の日記には何が書かれていたのでしょうか。
6. ジャーナルには何が書かれていたのでしょうか?
7. 書店の隠し通路は、エミリーをどこへ導いたのか?
8. 立派なオークの木の根元で、エミリーは何を見つけたのだろう。
9. 木箱の中に入っていた手書きのメモは、何を語っていたのでしょうか。
10. エミリーとアンダーソン氏は、書店の本当の魔法に何を悟ったのだろうか。

Cursed Artifact

In the heart of a forgotten temple, deep within a dense **jungle**, lay a cursed artifact. Legends whispered of its malevolent power and the misfortune that befell anyone who dared possess it. The artifact was said to be a small, intricately carved amulet, adorned with mysterious **symbols** and shimmering with an otherworldly glow. For centuries, it had remained hidden, its dark secrets guarded by the ancient spirits of the temple. One day, a fearless archaeologist named Dr. Amelia Carter stumbled upon the temple during her expedition. Drawn to its enigmatic aura, she entered the crumbling structure, determined to uncover its **mysteries**. Guided by her insatiable curiosity, Amelia navigated the labyrinthine corridors until she stumbled upon the sacred **chamber** that housed the cursed artifact.

As Amelia reached out to touch the amulet, a shiver ran down her **spine**. She hesitated for a moment, but the allure of unlocking the secrets within was too powerful to **resist**. With trembling hands, she grasped the amulet, unaware of the dark forces that awakened with her touch. From that moment on, Amelia's life took a dramatic turn. Strange occurrences plagued her **existence**. Misfortune befell her at every step, as if the world itself had turned against her. Her once promising career

呪われたアーティファクト

密林の奥深く、忘れられた寺院の中心には、呪われた芸術品があった。このアーティファクトには、邪悪な力と、それを手にした者に降りかかる災難の伝説が囁かれていた。そのアーティファクトは、複雑な彫刻が施された小さなお守りで、神秘的な**シンボル**で飾られ、別世界のような輝きを放っているという。何世紀もの間、その秘密は寺院の古代の精霊によって守られ、隠されたままだった。ある日、大胆不敵な考古学者アメリア・カーター博士が、探検中にこの神殿を偶然発見する。その謎めいたオーラに惹かれた彼女は、その**謎を**解き明かそうと、崩れかけた建造物の中に入っていく。好奇心旺盛なアメリアは、迷路のような回廊を進み、呪われた遺物が納められている聖なる**部屋に辿り着く**。

アメリアがその魔除けに手を伸ばしたとき、**背筋がゾクゾクした**。一瞬ためらったが、秘密を解き明かすという魅力に**抗う**ことはできなかった。アメリアは震える手でアミュレットを握りしめ、触れることで目覚める闇の力に気づかなかった。その瞬間から、アメリアの人生は劇的に変化していった。奇妙な現象に悩まされるように**なった**。まるで世界が敵に回ったかのように、あらゆる場面で災難に見舞われた。かつての有望なキャリアは崩れ、人間関係は壊れ、彼女は自分の世界から追放されるようになった。呪いに取り憑かれたアメリアは、呪いを解くための絶望的な探求に乗り出した。古文書を読み漁り、神秘主義者に教えを請うが、すべて無駄であった。呪いは**不滅の**ようで、その力は日を追うごとに強くなっていった。

crumbled, relationships shattered, and she became an outcast in her own world. Haunted by the curse, Amelia embarked on a desperate quest to break its grip. She consulted ancient texts and sought the guidance of wise mystics, but all in vain. The curse seemed **indestructible**, its power growing stronger with each passing day.

Driven to the brink of despair, Amelia discovered a **glimmer** of hope in an old journal. It spoke of a hidden ritual, passed down through generations, capable of breaking the curse. With renewed **determination**, Amelia journeyed to a remote village nestled in the mountains, home to the last living descendant of the ancient temple guardians. Under the guidance of the wise elder, Amelia underwent a grueling trial of courage and sacrifice. She ventured into the depths of her fears, facing the demons within her soul. Through sheer determination and the unwavering belief in her own **redemption**, Amelia emerged victorious. As the final remnants of the curse dissolved, Amelia felt a weight lift from her **shoulders**. She had overcome the malevolent power that had plagued her existence. With newfound wisdom, she vowed to protect others from the cursed artifact, to prevent its darkness from inflicting further harm.

絶望の淵に立たされたアメリアは、一冊の古い日記に希望の光を見出す。そこには、何世代にもわたって受け継がれてきた、呪いを解くための隠された儀式のことが書かれていた。アメリアは決意を新たに、山奥の村に向かった。そこには、古代神殿の守護者の最後の子孫が住んでいた。賢者の指導のもと、アメリアは勇気と犠牲を伴う過酷な試練に挑む。恐怖のどん底に突き落とされ、心の中の悪魔と向き合いました。アメリアは、強い決意と、自分自身の救済を信じる揺るぎない信念によって、勝利を収めました。呪いの残滓が消え、アメリアは肩の荷が下りるのを感じた。自分の存在を苦しめていた邪悪な力を克服したのだ。アメリアは新たな知恵を得たことで、呪われたアーティファクトから人々を守り、その闇がこれ以上害を及ぼさないようにすることを誓った。

Comprehension Questions

1. What is the cursed artifact described as in the text?

2. Where was the cursed artifact hidden?

3. What happened to anyone who possessed the cursed artifact?

4. Who is the protagonist of the story and what is her profession?

5. What compelled Dr. Amelia Carter to enter the temple and touch the amulet?

6. How did Amelia's life change after she touched the cursed artifact?

7. What attempts did Amelia make to break the curse?

8. Where did Amelia find a glimmer of hope to break the curse?

9. Who guided Amelia in her quest to break the curse?

10. How did Amelia ultimately overcome the curse?

理解度チェック問題

1. 本文中にある呪われた人工物とは、どのようなものだと説明されているのでしょうか?
2. 呪われたアーティファクトはどこに隠されていたのか?
3. 呪われたアーティファクトを手にした者はどうなったのか?
4. この物語の主人公は誰で、どんな職業なのか?
5. アメリア・カーター博士は、なぜ神殿に入り、お守りに触れなければならなかったのでしょうか。
6. 呪われたアーティファクトに触れたことで、アメリアの人生はどう変化したのか?
7. アメリアは呪いを解くためにどんな試みをしたのでしょうか?
8. アメリアはどこで呪いを解く希望の光を見出したのか。
9. 呪いを解くためにアメリアを導いてくれたのは誰なのか?
10. アメリアは最終的にどのように呪いを克服したのでしょうか?

The Masked Stranger

The small village of Oakwood was known for its tight-knit **community** and peaceful atmosphere. Life carried on as usual for the villagers, until one fateful day when a mysterious masked stranger arrived. The stranger's face was hidden beneath a black mask, leaving only their piercing eyes **visible**. Whispers spread throughout the village, and curiosity mixed with fear hung in the air. The masked stranger moved with an air of grace and mystery. They never spoke a word, communicating only through gestures and expressions. Each day, the stranger would wander through the village, observing the villagers' **activities** with an intensity that made some uneasy. Some believed the stranger was a harbinger of misfortune, while others were intrigued by the enigmatic figure. As days turned into weeks, the villagers began to notice a change within **themselves**. The presence of the masked stranger seemed to awaken something deep within their souls. Creativity flourished, and new ideas emerged.

Painters crafted masterpieces, musicians composed haunting **melodies**, and writers penned mesmerizing stories. The village blossomed with a renewed sense of inspiration and purpose.

仮面のストレンジャー

小さな村、オークウッドは、結束の固いコミュニティと穏やかな雰囲気で知られていた。しかし、ある日、謎の覆面をした見知らぬ男がやってくる。見知らぬ男は黒いマスクで顔を隠しており、鋭い**目だけが見えている**。村人たちの間では、好奇心や恐怖心が渦巻いていた。仮面をつけた見知らぬ男は、優雅で神秘的な雰囲気を漂わせながら動いていた。彼らは一言も話さず、身振り手振りと表情だけで意思疎通を図った。毎日、村の中を歩き回り、村人たちの**行動を**熱心に観察していた。ある者は災いの前触れだと思い、またある者は謎めいたその人物に興味を持った。そして、数日、数週間と経つうちに、村人たちは**自分たちの変化に気づき始めた**。仮面をかぶった見知らぬ男の存在が、彼らの心の奥底にある何かを呼び覚ますように思えたのだ。そして、創造性が生まれ、新しいアイデアが生まれるようになった。

画家は名画を描き、音楽家は心に響く**メロディーを奏**で、作家は魅惑的な物語を綴った。村は新たなインスピレーションと目的意識で花開いた。ある晩、村の広場に集まっていた少女イライザは、仮面をつけた見知らぬ男に近づいていった。彼女は震える手で、**手作りの小さな**仮面を贈り物にした。見知らぬ男はうなずきながらその仮面を受け取り、その目は感謝で輝いていた。イライザは、言葉を超えて、無言の了解を得たのだ。夜が更けるにつれ、村人たちは仮面をつけた**見知らぬ人**の微妙な変化に気がついた。村人たちの動きはより滑らかになり、その仕草は新たな温もりを伝えていた。そして、皆を誘

One evening, during a festive gathering in the village square, a young girl named Eliza approached the masked stranger. With a trembling hand, she offered a small **handcrafted** mask as a gift. The stranger accepted the mask with a nod, their eyes gleaming with gratitude. Eliza sensed a connection, a silent understanding that transcended words. As the night wore on, the villagers noticed a subtle change in the masked **stranger**. Their movements became more fluid, their gestures conveying a newfound warmth. And then, with a gesture that invited everyone to follow, the stranger led them to an abandoned **theater** on the outskirts of the village.

Within the theater's dilapidated walls, the villagers discovered a **hidden** treasure trove of costumes, props, and instruments. The masked stranger encouraged them to embrace their hidden **desires** and fears, to step into the roles they had longed to play. The theater came alive with laughter, tears, and a whirlwind of emotions as the villagers indulged in their passions. Days turned into months, and the masked stranger became an integral part of the village. They became a **symbol** of liberation, reminding the villagers to shed their inhibitions and embrace their true selves. The once-muted village now thrived with vibrant expressions of art and individuality. Eventually, the masked **stranger** departed as silently as they had arrived, leaving behind a transformed village. The memories of their presence lingered, forever etched in the hearts of the villagers.

うような仕草で、村の外れにある廃墟のような**劇場に案内してくれた。**

荒廃した劇場の壁の中に、村人たちは衣装、小道具、楽器の宝庫を発見した。仮面をかぶった見知らぬ男は、村人たちに、自分の隠れた欲望や恐怖を受け入れ、憧れの役になりきるように促した。劇場は笑いと涙に包まれ、村人たちの情熱が渦巻いた。日々は月日を経て、仮面をつけた見知らぬ人は、村に欠かせない存在となった。そして、村人たちに抑制を解き放ち、本当の自分を受け入れることを思い出させる、解放の**シンボルとなった。**かつては静かだった村は、芸術と個性を生き生きと表現することで繁栄していった。やがて、仮面をつけた**見知らぬ男たちは、**到着したときと同じように静かに去っていき、変わり果てた村を後にした。しかし、彼らの存在は、村人たちの心に永遠に刻まれた。

Comprehension Questions

1. What was the initial reaction of the villagers when the masked stranger arrived?

2. How did the masked stranger communicate with the villagers?

3. What effect did the presence of the masked stranger have on the villagers' creativity?

4. What types of art forms flourished in the village after the arrival of the masked stranger?

5. Who offered a small handcrafted mask as a gift to the stranger?

6. What change did the villagers notice in the masked stranger as the night wore on?

7. Where did the stranger lead the villagers?

8. What did the villagers discover within the abandoned theater?

9. How did the masked stranger encourage the villagers to express themselves?

10. How did the masked stranger's departure impact the village?

理解度チェック問題

1. 仮面をつけた見知らぬ男がやってきたとき、村人たちは最初にどんな反応をしたのでしょうか。
2. 仮面をかぶった見知らぬ人は、村人たちとどのようにコミュニケーションをとったのでしょうか。
3. 仮面をつけた見知らぬ人の存在は、村人たちの創造性にどのような影響を与えたのでしょうか。
4. 仮面をつけたよそ者がやってきた後、村ではどのような芸術が盛んになったのでしょうか。
5. 見知らぬ人に、手作りの小さなマスクをプレゼントしたのは誰ですか?
6. 夜が更けるにつれ、村人たちは仮面をつけた見知らぬ男にどんな変化を感じたのだろうか。
7. 見知らぬ人は村人たちをどこに案内したのでしょうか。
8. 廃墟と化した劇場の中で、村人たちは何を発見したのだろうか。
9. 仮面をかぶった見知らぬ人は、村人たちにどのように自己表現を促したのでしょうか。
10. 仮面をかぶったよそ者の出発は、村にどのような影響を与えたのだろうか。

Star-Crossed Lovers

In the enchanting town of Verona, two young souls found themselves **entangled** in a love that transcended time and defied the boundaries of their feuding families. Romeo, a passionate and impulsive young man, was the son of the esteemed Montagues. Juliet, a charming and free-spirited **maiden**, belonged to the noble Capulets. Their families were locked in a bitter rivalry, a feud that had lasted for generations. Yet, amidst the chaos and animosity, Romeo and Juliet's hearts beat as one. Their love blossomed in secret. Under the starry night sky, they would meet at a hidden **garden**, whispering sweet words of devotion. Their forbidden romance became a solace, a refuge from the world that sought to keep them apart. They dreamt of a future where their families' animosity would fade away, where they could **embrace** their love without fear.

But fate had other plans. As rumors spread, Juliet's father arranged for her to be wed to a noble suitor, Paris. Desperate to escape this fate, Juliet sought the **guidance** of Friar Laurence, a wise and compassionate mentor. Together, they devised a daring plan to unite the star-crossed lovers in **matrimony**. On the eve of her wedding to Paris, Juliet consumed a sleeping potion, a concoction that would make her appear lifeless for a

スタークロスド・ラバーズ

魅惑的なヴェローナの町で、2人の若い魂が、時代を超え、確執のある家族の境界を越えて、愛に**絡め取られているのを**発見したのです。情熱的で衝動的な青年ロミオは、尊敬するモンタギュー家の息子だった。ジュリエットは自由奔放で魅力的な**乙女で**、高貴なキャピュレット家に属していた。両家は代々続く確執の中で、激しく対立していた。しかし、ロミオとジュリエットの心は、混乱と反感の中でひとつになった。二人の愛は密かに花開いた。星空の下、二人は秘密の**花園で**出会い、甘い言葉を囁きながら愛を育んだ。禁断の恋は、二人を引き離そうとする世間からの逃避行となり、慰めとなった。家族の反感が消え、安心して愛を**育むことができる未来を夢見た。**

しかし、運命は別の計画を立てていた。噂が広まり、ジュリエットの父は彼女を高貴な求婚者パリスと結婚させるように仕向けたのだ。この運命から逃れたいジュリエットは、賢くて思いやりのあるローレンス修道士に**教えを請う。**ジュリエットはローレンス修道士に教えを請い、**二人の仲を取り持つ**ために大胆な計画を立てた。パリスとの結婚式の前夜、ジュリエットは睡眠薬を飲み、しばらくの間、生気を失っているように見せる。ロミオはジュリエットの死の知らせを受け、彼女を墓から救い出し、愛と**自由な**生活へと連れ出す計画だった。しかし、その計画を知らないロミオが墓に到着し、ジュリエットの無残な姿を見たとき、悲劇は起こった。悲しみに打ちひしがれたロミオは、ジュリエットと一緒に死のうと、**毒の入った**小瓶を飲み干した。

brief period. The plan was for Romeo to receive news of her apparent death and rescue her from her tomb, whisking her away to a life of love and **freedom**. However, tragedy struck when Romeo, unaware of the plan, arrived at the tomb and saw Juliet's lifeless form. Consumed by grief, he drank a vial of **poison**, hoping to join her in death.

As Juliet awoke from her slumber, she discovered Romeo's lifeless body beside her. Overwhelmed with **sorrow**, she kissed his lips, hoping to find a taste of the love they once shared. In that moment, Juliet's heart stopped beating, and she joined her beloved in eternal sleep. The tragic tale of Romeo and Juliet shook the foundations of Verona. The feuding **families**, torn apart by the loss of their children, realized the folly of their enmity. In grief and remorse, they vowed to end the rivalry and honor the memory of the star-crossed lovers. From that day forward, the Montagues and Capulets lived side by side in **peace**. The tale of Romeo and Juliet became a legend, a reminder of the power of love and the tragic **consequences** of hatred.

ジュリエットが眠りから覚めると、傍らにロミオの亡骸があった。**悲しみに打ち**ひしがれたジュリエットは、かつての愛を取り戻そうと、彼の唇にキスをした。その瞬間、ジュリエットの心臓は止まり、愛する人と永遠の眠りにつきました。ロミオとジュリエットの悲劇的な物語は、ヴェローナの根幹を揺るがした。対立していた**一族は**、子供を失ったことで引き裂かれ、敵対することの愚かさを思い知った。悲しみと自責の念に駆られた一族は、対立関係を解消し、すれ違った恋人たちの思い出を称えることを誓った。その日以来、モンタギュー家とキャピュレット家は**平和に共存する**ようになった。ロミオとジュリエットの物語は伝説となり、愛の力と憎しみの悲劇的な**結末を**思い起こさせるものとなった。

Comprehension Questions

1. Who were the two young lovers in the story?

2. What were the names of their feuding families?

3. Where did Romeo and Juliet meet in secret?

4. What did Juliet's father arrange for her?

5. Who did Juliet seek guidance from to escape her fate?

6. What was the plan devised by Juliet and Friar Laurence?

7. What did Juliet consume on the eve of her wedding?

8. What was Romeo's reaction when he saw Juliet's lifeless form in the tomb?

9. What did Juliet do when she woke up from her slumber?

10. How did the tragedy of Romeo and Juliet affect the feuding families?

理解度チェック問題

1. 物語に登場する若い二人の恋人は誰だったのでしょうか?
2. 確執のあった家族の名前は何だったのでしょうか?
3. ロミオとジュリエットはどこで密会したのでしょうか?
4. ジュリエットの父は何を手配したのでしょうか。
5. ジュリエットは自分の運命から逃れるために、誰に教えを請うたのか。
6. ジュリエットと修道士ローランスが考えた計画とは?
7. ジュリエットは結婚式の前夜に何を消費したのか?
8. 墓の中でジュリエットの生気のない姿を見たロミオは、どんな反応をしたのでしょうか。
9. 眠りから覚めたジュリエットはどうしたのでしょう?
10. ロミオとジュリエット』の悲劇は、確執のある家族にどのような影響を与えたのでしょうか。

Moonlit Masquerade

In the enchanting city of Venaria, nestled in the hills of Italy, there existed a grand **mansion** known as Villa di Luna. The mansion was renowned for its lavish parties and extravagant celebrations. But once a year, on the night of the full **moon**, something truly magical took place—the Moonlit Masquerade. It was an event shrouded in mystery, where guests arrived adorned in exquisite masks and attire, their true identities **concealed**. On one particular moonlit night, a young woman named Isabella received an invitation to the Moonlit Masquerade. Intrigued by the allure of the event, she eagerly accepted, her heart fluttering with anticipation. As the night arrived, Isabella donned a shimmering gown, her mask an **intricate** creation of silver and lace. She arrived at Villa di Luna, mesmerized by the sight that greeted her—a garden transformed into a realm of enchantment, bathed in the soft glow of moonlight.

Isabella found herself immersed in a whirlwind of **music**, laughter, and whispers of love. The air was filled with a sense of mystique as guests danced and mingled, their identities hidden behind a myriad of masks. Isabella danced with a masked stranger, their **movements** perfectly synchronized, as

ムーンリット・マスカレード

イタリアの丘陵地帯に位置する魅惑の街ヴェナリアに、ヴィラ・ディ・ルナという**大邸宅があった**。この邸宅では、豪華なパーティーが催されることで有名であった。しかし、年に一度、**満月の夜に行われる**「月夜の仮面舞踏会」は、実に幻想的なものだった。仮面や衣装を身にまとい、**正体を隠して参加する謎に包まれたイベントだ**。ある月夜の晩、イザベラという若い女性のもとに「月夜の仮面舞踏会」の招待状が届きました。その魅力に惹かれたイザベラは、期待に胸を膨らませながら快諾した。夜が明けると、イザベラはきらめくガウンを身にまとい、銀とレースで**精巧に**作られた仮面をつけた。月明かりに照らされた庭は、まさに魅惑の世界。

イザベラは、音楽と笑い声、そして愛のささやきの渦の中に身を置いていることに気づいた。ゲストは無数のマスクで正体を隠しながら踊り、交流し、空気は神秘的な雰囲気に包まれた。イザベラは仮面をつけた見知らぬ男と踊り、その**動きは**まるで月の優しい揺れに導かれるかのように完全にシンクロしていた。まるで月の穏やかな揺れに導かれるように、2人の動きは完全にシンクロし、目を見て語り合い、言葉を超えた絆が生まれた。その一瞬に、イザベラは二人の間に言い知れぬ絆が生まれるのを感じた。夜が更けるにつれ、イザベラは仮面をつけた見知らぬ男の魅力と気品に**魅了されていった**。二人は物語や夢、秘密を共有し、信頼と親密さのタペストリーを織り上げていった。まるで時が止まったかのように、屋敷の外の世界は**無意味に消えていった**。しかし、夜が最高潮に達したとき、覆面をした見知らぬ男は人ごみの中

if guided by the moon's gentle sway. They spoke with their eyes, their connection transcending words. In that fleeting moment, Isabella felt an inexplicable bond forming between them. As the night wore on, Isabella grew **captivated** by the masked stranger's charm and grace. They shared stories, dreams, and secrets, weaving a tapestry of trust and intimacy. It was as though time stood still, the world outside the mansion fading away into **insignificance**. But just as the night reached its peak, the masked stranger disappeared into the crowd, leaving Isabella yearning for more.

Days turned into weeks, and Isabella's heart remained haunted by the **memory** of the Moonlit Masquerade. Determined to uncover the identity of her masked companion, she embarked on a quest. She sought clues, followed whispers, and delved into the secrets of the city. Through her relentless **pursuit**, Isabella discovered that the masked stranger was none other than Alessandro, a talented artist known for his evocative paintings. With newfound knowledge, Isabella sought Alessandro in his **studio**. Their reunion was filled with emotions—joy, longing, and a sense of completion. Their masks now discarded, they bared their souls to one another. Inspired by their connection, Alessandro created a **masterpiece**, capturing the essence of their moonlit encounter.

に消えてしまった。

イザベラの心は、月夜のマスカレードの**記憶に取りつか
れたまま**だった。仮面をつけた仲間の正体を突き止めよ
うと決意した彼女は、旅に出た。手がかりを探し、ささ
やきを追い、街の秘密を探る。その結果、イザベラは、
仮面をかぶった見知らぬ男がアレッサンドロであること
を突き止めた。アレッサンドロは、情感豊かな絵で知ら
れる才能ある画家だった。そして、イザベラはアレッサ
ンドロの**アトリエを訪ねる**。二人の再会は、喜びと憧
れ、そして達成感で満たされた。仮面を捨てた二人は、
互いの魂をむき出しにした。アレッサンドロは、二人の
つながりに触発され、月夜の出会いの本質をとらえた**傑
作を**制作しました。

Comprehension Questions

1. What was the name of the grand mansion in Venaria known for its extravagant celebrations?

2. What special event took place at Villa di Luna once a year?

3. How did Isabella feel when she received an invitation to the Moonlit Masquerade?

4. Describe Isabella's attire for the Moonlit Masquerade.

5. How did Isabella feel when she arrived at Villa di Luna?

6. How did the masked stranger and Isabella communicate with each other?

7. What emotions did Isabella experience as she spent time with the masked stranger?

8. What happened to the masked stranger just as the night reached its peak?

9. What did Isabella do after the Moonlit Masquerade to uncover the identity of the masked stranger?

10. Who did Isabella discover the masked stranger's true identity to be, and what was his profession?

理解度チェック問題

1. 豪華な祝宴で知られるヴェナリアの大邸宅の名前は何だったのか?

2. ヴィラ・ディ・ルナで1年に1度行われた特別なイベントとは?

3. ムーンリット・マスカレードの招待状を受け取ったイザベラは、どのような気持ちだったのでしょうか。

4. 月夜のマスカレードでのイザベラの服装について説明してください。

5. ヴィラ・ディ・ルナに到着したイザベラは、どんな気持ちでいたのでしょうか?

6. 仮面の見知らぬ人とイザベラは、どのようにコミュニケーションをとっていたのでしょうか。

7. イザベラは仮面をつけた見知らぬ人と過ごす中で、どんな感情を抱いたのでしょうか。

8. 夜が最高潮に達したとき、仮面をつけた見知らぬ男に何が起こったのか?

9. 月夜のマスカレードの後、イザベラが仮面をつけた見知らぬ男の正体を暴くためにしたこととは?

10. イザベラは仮面をつけた見知らぬ男の正体を突き止め、その職業は何だったのか。

Enchanted Forest

Deep within the heart of the Enchanted Forest, where sunlight filtered through the dense canopy, a world of magic and wonder unfolded. It was a place where the ordinary became **extraordinary**, and dreams transformed into reality. The Enchanted Forest was home to mythical creatures, talking animals, and ancient spirits who guarded its secrets. In this mystical realm, a young girl named Lily embarked on an **adventure**. With wide-eyed wonder, she ventured deeper into the forest, the scent of moss and wildflowers filling her senses. She was drawn to the ethereal glow emanating from a cluster of ancient trees. As she approached, she discovered a hidden **pathway**, veiled by vines and overgrown foliage. Curiosity guiding her, Lily followed the path, her heart pounding with **anticipation**. With each step, the air grew thick with enchantment. Whispers of the wind carried melodies of the forest, and sunbeams danced upon the emerald leaves.

As Lily walked, she encountered magical **creatures**. A mischievous fairy fluttered by, leaving a trail of sparkling dust in her wake. A wise old owl perched on a branch, offering cryptic riddles. Lily giggled as a playful squirrel tugged on her dress, inviting her to join in its **acrobatic** antics. Deeper

エンチャンテッド・フォレスト

魔法にかけられた森の奥深く、鬱蒼とした樹木の間から太陽の光が差し込むと、そこには魔法と驚異の世界が広がっていました。そこは、日常が**非日常となり**、夢が現実となる場所でした。魔法にかけられた森には、神話に登場する生き物や、しゃべる動物、秘密を守る古代の精霊が住んでいました。この神秘的な世界で、リリーという名の少女が**冒険の旅に出ます**。苔や野草の香りに包まれながら、目を輝かせて森の奥へ奥へと進んでいく。そして、古木の群生から放たれる幽玄な光に惹かれた。近づくと、つる植物や生い茂った葉で覆われた、隠れた**小道を発見**した。好奇心に駆られたリリーは、**期待に胸を**躍らせながら、その道を進んでいく。一歩一歩進むたびに、空気は魔法に包まれたように濃くなっていく。風のささやきは森のメロディーを運び、太陽の光はエメラルドの葉の上で踊る。

リリーは歩いていると、不思議な**生き物**に出会います。いたずら好きな妖精は、キラキラとした粉の跡を残しながら、ひらひらと通り過ぎていった。賢いフクロウは枝に止まり、謎かけをする。リリーは、遊び好きなリスに服を引っ張られ、その**アクロバティックな**動きに誘われ、思わず笑ってしまった。森の奥に進むと、リリーは人里離れた空き地に出くわした。その中央には荘厳な滝があり、流れ落ちる水は銀のように輝いていた。その滝の水音に魅せられたリリーは、思わず指先を滝の水面に浸した。指が水面に触れた瞬間、リリーの体にエネルギーが走った。リリーは目を見開き、森が活気づくのを目の当たりにした。花は鮮やかに咲き誇り、木々は古代の

into the forest, Lily stumbled upon a secluded clearing. In the center stood a majestic waterfall, its cascading waters glistening like liquid silver. The sound of its soothing melody enchanted her, and she couldn't resist the temptation to dip her fingertips into the **crystalline** pool. As her fingers touched the water, a surge of energy coursed through Lily's body. Her eyes widened as she witnessed the forest coming alive. Flowers bloomed in vibrant hues, and trees whispered ancient tales. The forest acknowledged her presence, accepting her as part of its enchanting **tapestry**.

Lily's heart swelled with gratitude, and she vowed to protect and cherish the Enchanted Forest. She returned to her **village**, sharing tales of its magic, hoping to inspire others to preserve the **beauty** of nature. Years passed, and Lily, now an old woman, returned to the Enchanted Forest. The forest embraced her with open arms, as if time had stood still. She marveled at the same hidden **pathway**, the same playful creatures, and the same majestic waterfall. As she breathed in the familiar scents and listened to the forest's **symphony**, Lily felt a deep sense of peace. The Enchanted Forest had become a part of her, and she had become a part of it.

物語をささやく。森は彼女の存在を認め、その魅惑的な**タペストリー**の一部として受け入れてくれたのだ。

リリーは感謝の気持ちで胸がいっぱいになり、魔法の森を守り、大切にすることを誓いました。そして、**村に戻り**、魔法の物語を語り、**美しい自然を守ろう**とする人々の心を動かすのでした。年月が経ち、老婆となったリリーは再び魔法の森に戻った。まるで時間が止まってしまったかのように、森は彼女を優しく包み込んだ。リリーは、同じように隠された**小道**、同じように愉快な生き物、同じように雄大な滝に驚嘆した。嗅ぎ慣れた香りを吸い込み、森の**シンフォニーに耳を傾けながら**、リリーは深い安らぎを覚えた。魔法の森は彼女の一部となり、彼女もまたその一部となったのだ。

Comprehension Questions

1. Where did Lily embark on her adventure?

2. What kind of creatures did Lily encounter in the Enchanted Forest?

3. What was the allure that drew Lily deeper into the forest?

4. How did the forest respond to Lily's presence?

5. Describe the scene in the secluded clearing that Lily discovered.

6. What happened when Lily touched the water in the crystalline pool?

7. What did Lily vow to do after her experience in the Enchanted Forest?

8. How did the Enchanted Forest embrace Lily when she returned as an old woman?

9. What did Lily feel as she listened to the forest's symphony?

10. How did Lily's relationship with the Enchanted Forest evolve over time?

理解度チェック問題

1. リリーはどこで冒険の旅に出たのでしょうか?
2. リリーは「魔法の森」でどんな生き物に出会ったのでしょう?
3. リリーを森の奥に引き込んだ魅力は何だったのか。
4. リリーの存在に、森はどう反応したのだろう。
5. リリーが発見した人里離れた空き地の情景を描写する。
6. リリーが水晶のプールの水に触れたとき、何が起こったのか。
7. 魔法の森での体験を経て、リリーは何を誓ったのか。
8. 老婆になって戻ってきたリリーを、魔法の森はどのように受け入れたのでしょうか。
9. 森のシンフォニーを聴きながら、リリーは何を感じたのだろう。
10. リリーと「魔法の森」の関係は、時代とともにどのように変化していったのでしょうか。

The Solitary Island

The Solitary Island stood in the middle of a vast, **mysterious** ocean, shrouded in an ethereal mist. It was a place untouched by time and forgotten by the world. Legends whispered of its mystical powers, while sailors spoke of its enchanting beauty. But only a few dared to **venture** to its shores, for the island held a secret—a secret known only to those who embraced solitude. One such traveler was a young woman named Amelia. Haunted by the noise and chaos of civilization, she longed for a place of tranquility and introspection. Driven by an unquenchable curiosity, Amelia set sail towards the Solitary Island, seeking solace in its **isolation**. As her boat approached the shores, a sense of calm washed over her. The island welcomed her with open arms, as if it had been waiting for her **arrival**.

Amelia stepped onto the sandy beach, her bare feet sinking into the soft grains. The air was crisp, carrying the scent of **wildflowers** and the gentle melody of waves crashing against the rocks. She wandered through dense forests, their emerald foliage whispering ancient **wisdom**. In meadows adorned with vibrant blooms, she found solace in the delicate embrace of nature. Days turned into weeks, and Amelia embraced the

孤島（こじま

広大で**神秘的な**海の真ん中に、幽玄な霧に包まれた孤島がある。そこは、時が経つのも忘れて、世界から忘れ去られた場所だった。その神秘的な力は伝説として語られ、船乗りたちはその魅惑的な美しさを語っていた。この島には、孤独を愛する者だけが知る秘密があったのだ。その一人が、アメリアという名の若い女性だった。文明の喧噪に取り憑かれた彼女は、静寂と内省に満ちた場所に憧れていた。好奇心旺盛なアメリアは、**孤島に癒し**を求め、船出した。船が海岸に近づくにつれ、アメリアは穏やかな気持ちになった。島は、まるで彼女の**到着を待っていたかのように**、両手を広げて迎えてくれた。

アメリアは砂浜に足を踏み入れ、素足で柔らかな粒に沈み込んだ。空気は澄んでいて、**野草の香り**と岩に打ち付ける波の穏やかな旋律が伝わってくる。エメラルド色の葉が古代の**知恵をささやく**、うっそうとした森を歩き回る。エメラルドの葉が古代の知恵を囁き、鮮やかな花が咲き乱れる草原では、繊細な自然の抱擁に安らぎを覚えた。アメリアは、**周囲の**シンプルな環境に溶け込むように、日を重ね、週を重ねた。隠された洞窟を発見し、その壁には暗闇を照らすクリスタルの煌めきがあった。透明なラグーンで泳ぎ、まるで恋人のように肌を撫でた。月明かりの下で、波の**リズムに合わせて**体を動かす。

しかし、その静けさの中で、アメリアの心には憧れのようなものが芽生えていた。島は息を呑むほど美しいが、人と人との**つながりが希薄**だった。気の合う仲間との会話や笑いが欲しくなった。孤独が、まるで錨のように重

simplicity of her **surroundings**. She discovered hidden caves, their walls adorned with shimmering crystals that illuminated the darkness. She swam in crystal-clear lagoons, feeling the water caress her skin like a lover's touch. She danced under the moonlight, her body moving in sync with the **rhythm** of the waves.

But amidst the serenity, a sense of longing crept into Amelia's heart. The island, although breathtaking, was devoid of human **connection**. She yearned for conversation, for laughter shared with kindred souls. Her solitude began to feel heavy, like an anchor weighing her down. One night, as Amelia gazed at the star-studded sky, she made a **decision**. She would leave the Solitary Island and return to the world she had left behind. With a heavy heart, she bid farewell to the island that had nurtured her **spirit**. But as her boat sailed away, a bittersweet smile played on her lips, for she carried the memories of the island's tranquility within her. Years passed, and the Solitary Island remained a distant memory. Amelia had found her place in the bustling city, surrounded by the chaos she had once sought to **escape**. But deep within her soul, the island's tranquility remained, a beacon of solace in times of chaos.

く感じられるようになった。ある夜、満天の星空を眺めながら、アメリアはある**決意をした**。孤島を出て、自分が残してきた世界に戻ろう。自分の**心を育んでくれた島**に、重い気持ちで別れを告げた。しかし、船出するとき、彼女の唇にはほろ苦い笑みが浮かんでいた。年月は流れ、孤島は遠い思い出となった。アメリアは、かつて**逃れ**ようとした混沌に包まれた都会の喧騒の中で、自分の居場所を見つけた。しかし、彼女の心の奥底には、島の静けさが残っていた。

Comprehension Questions

1. Where is the Solitary Island located?

2. What did legends say about the Solitary Island?

3. Why did Amelia decide to set sail towards the Solitary Island?

4. How did Amelia feel when her boat approached the shores of the island?

5. What were some of the natural elements that Amelia experienced on the island?

6. How did Amelia find solace in nature on the island?

7. What did Amelia discover in the hidden caves on the island?

8. How did Amelia feel about the lack of human connection on the island?

9. What made Amelia decide to leave the Solitary Island?

10. How did Amelia carry the memories of the island's tranquility with her in the bustling city?

理解度チェック問題

1. 孤島はどこにあるのですか?
2. 孤島の伝説はどうだった?
3. なぜアメリアは孤島に向かって出航することにしたのか?
4. 船が島の海岸に近づいたとき、アメリアはどんな気持ちだったのだろう。
5. アメリアさんが島で体験した自然はどのようなものだったのでしょうか。
6. アメリアは、島でどのように自然の中で安らぎを得たのでしょうか。
7. アメリアは島の隠された洞窟で何を発見したのだろう。
8. アメリアは、島で人と人とのつながりがないことをどう感じていたのでしょうか。
9. アメリアはなぜ孤島を出ようと思ったのか?
10. アメリアは、島の静けさの記憶を、喧騒の都会でどのように持ち運んだのだろうか。

A Glimpse of Eternity

In a small, quaint town nestled in the **valleys**, a curious young boy named Lucas roamed the streets with wonder in his eyes. He had always been captivated by stories of the supernatural, and his imagination ran wild with tales of magic and mystery. One **fateful** day, as Lucas explored the outskirts of town, he stumbled upon an ancient, crumbling book hidden within the depths of an old library. The book beckoned to him, its leather cover worn and weathered. Intrigued, Lucas gingerly opened its pages and was immediately transported into a world beyond his **wildest** dreams. The book unveiled secrets of an extraordinary portal that led to realms unknown, offering a glimpse of eternity. Driven by an insatiable curiosity, Lucas followed the book's instructions to the letter. He found himself in a secluded grove, where moonlight filtered through a dense **canopy**, casting an ethereal glow upon the forest floor.

Before him stood a colossal, ornate door, adorned with intricate **carvings** and symbols. With bated breath, Lucas pushed the door open, revealing a breathtaking sight. He stepped into a realm untouched by time, where the air crackled with magic.

永遠を垣間見る

渓谷に囲まれた小さな町で、ルーカスという名の好奇心旺盛な少年は、目を輝かせて通りを歩き回っていました。彼はいつも超自然的な話に魅了され、魔法と神秘の物語に想像を膨らませていた。ある日、ルーカスは町外れにある古い図書館の奥で、古くて崩れそうな本に出会いました。その本は、革の表紙が擦り切れて風化しており、手招きしているようだった。ルーカスは興味深げにページを開くと、たちまち想像を絶する世界へと誘われた。その本には、未知の世界へと続く特別な扉の秘密が書かれており、永遠を垣間見ることができた。ルーカスは飽くなき好奇心に駆られ、その本の指示に従った。すると、そこは人里離れた木立の中。鬱蒼とした樹木の間から月明かりが差し込み、林床に幽玄な輝きを放っていた。

目の前には、複雑な彫刻や記号で飾られた巨大な扉が立っていた。ルーカスは固唾を飲んで扉を開けると、そこには息を呑むような光景が広がっていた。ルーカスが足を踏み入れたのは、時が止まったような、魔法に満ちた世界だった。見渡す限り、鮮やかな花々が咲き乱れ、雄大な生き物が自由に動き回っている。ルーカスは、畏敬の念と驚きに包まれるのを感じた。そんな中、ルーカスは古代の精霊に出会い、忘れ去られた伝説やささやかな予言の話を聞かされた。ルーカスは、古代の精霊たちに導かれるまま、夕陽の色に輝く湖にたどり着いた。その

Endless fields of **vibrant** flowers stretched as far as the eye could see, and majestic creatures roamed freely. Lucas felt a surge of awe and wonder coursing through his veins. As he ventured deeper into this mystical realm, Lucas encountered ancient spirits who shared stories of forgotten legends and whispered **prophecies**. They guided him to a shimmering lake, its surface reflecting the colors of the setting sun. In the heart of the lake, Lucas caught a glimpse of eternity—a **breathtaking** vision of the past, present, and future merging into a single moment.

With newfound knowledge, Lucas returned to his town, forever changed by his journey. He shared the wisdom he had acquired, inspiring his fellow **townspeople** to embrace the extraordinary in the ordinary. The once-dull town transformed into a haven of creativity and **exploration**. Years passed, and Lucas grew old, but the memories of his adventure remained etched in his heart. On his final day, as he closed his eyes for the last time, Lucas felt a **profound** sense of peace. He knew that beyond this realm, he would embark on a new journey, venturing into the eternal unknown. And so, the tale of Lucas, the boy who caught a glimpse of eternity, lived on as a whispered legend, reminding generations to embrace the wonders that lie just beyond their **grasp**, waiting to be discovered.

湖の中心で、ルーカスは永遠を垣間見た。過去、現在、未来が一つの瞬間に融合した、**息を呑むようなビジョン**。

ルーカスは、この旅で得た知識をもとに、自分の町に戻ってきた。ルーカスは、自分が得た知恵を**町の人々に伝え**、日常の中にある非日常を受け入れるように促した。そして、かつての退屈な町は、創造と**探求の天国へと変わっていった**。年月は流れ、ルーカスは老いていったが、冒険の記憶は彼の心に刻まれたままだった。最後の日、最後に目を閉じたとき、ルーカスは**深い安らぎを覚**えた。この世界の先には、永遠の未知への新たな旅立ちが待っているのだと。そして、永遠を垣間見た少年ルーカスの物語は、伝説として語り継がれ、その先には、発見されるのを待っている不思議なものがあるのだと、世代を超えて語り継がれていった。

Comprehension Questions

1. What kind of town did Lucas live in?

2. What was Lucas's reaction to stories of the supernatural?

3. Where did Lucas find the ancient book?

4. How did the book appear to Lucas?

5. What did Lucas discover when he opened the book?

6. What did Lucas find in the secluded grove?

7. Describe the realm that Lucas entered through the ornate door.

8. What did Lucas witness in the shimmering lake?

9. How did Lucas's journey change his town?

10. How did Lucas feel on his final day, and what did he believe would happen next?

理解度チェック問題

1. ルーカスはどんな町に住んでいたのか?
2. 超常現象の話に対して、ルーカスはどのような反応を示したのでしょうか?
3. ルーカスはどこで古書を見つけたのだろう?
4. ルーカスには、この本がどのように映ったのでしょうか?
5. 本を開いたルーカスは何を発見したのだろうか。
6. ルーカスは人里離れた木立の中で何を見つけたのだろうか。
7. ルーカスが装飾された扉から入った領域を描写してください。
8. ルーカスは陽炎の湖で何を目撃したのだろうか。
9. ルーカスの旅は、彼の町をどう変えたのだろうか。
10. ルーカスは最後の日、どんな気持ちで、この先どうなると信じていたのだろうか。

Dancing Flames

In a small village nestled at the foot of a mighty **mountain**, there lived a young girl named Maya. She possessed a special gift—the ability to communicate with fire. Maya's heart would swell with joy whenever she witnessed the mesmerizing dance of flames, as if they were alive, speaking a **language** only she could understand. One chilly evening, as the villagers gathered around a crackling bonfire, Maya noticed something peculiar. The flames seemed different, vibrant and full of life. They leaped and twirled in an intricate **choreography**, captivating the onlookers. The villagers watched in awe as the flames took on the shapes of animals, creating a beautiful spectacle. Maya felt a strong urge to join the **dance**.

She stepped closer to the bonfire, feeling its warmth **embrace** her. With closed eyes, Maya extended her arms, mimicking the graceful movements of the flames. And to her astonishment, the flames **responded**, mirroring her every gesture. A wave of euphoria washed over Maya as she became one with the dancing flames. Together, they swayed and twirled, creating a mesmerizing symphony of light and heat. Word of Maya's **extraordinary** talent spread throughout the village, attracting curious spectators from far and wide. The villagers gathered

ダンシングフレイムス

大山のふもとにある小さな村に、マヤという名の少女が
住んでいた。マヤは、炎と対話できる特別な才能を持っ
ていました。マヤは、炎がまるで生きているかのよう
に、自分だけが理解できる**言葉を発しながら踊るのを見
る**たびに、喜びで胸がいっぱいになった。ある寒い夜、
村人たちが焚き火を囲んでいるとき、マヤは奇妙なこと
に気づきました。炎がいつもと違って、生き生きとして
いるのです。炎は躍動し、複雑に**絡み合い**、見る者を魅
了する。村人たちは、炎が動物の形をした美しい光景に
目を見張った。マヤは、この**踊り**に参加したいと強く思
った。

彼女は焚き火に近づき、その暖かさに**包まれるのを感じ
た**。目を閉じて、マヤは腕を伸ばし、炎の優雅な動きを
真似た。すると驚くことに、炎が彼女の**動きに合わせて
反応**した。マヤは幸福感に包まれ、踊る炎と一体となっ
た。光と熱のシンフォニーを奏でたのだ。マヤの才能は
村中に広まり、遠くから見物人がやってくるようになっ
た。村人たちは毎晩のように集まり、その光景を心待ち
にした。マヤの踊りは、喜びと驚きの源となり、村人た
ちの**絆を深めて**いきました。炎が舞うことで、体だけで
なく心も温かくなる。しかし、マヤの名声が高まるにつ
れ、妬みと欲も出てきた。マヤの名声が高まるにつれ
て、妬みと欲が生まれ、マヤの力を我が物にしようとす
る外敵が現れました。

彼らは彼女の才能を利用しようと、富と壮大な約束を提
供しました。マヤは自分の年齢以上に賢明で、彼らの**意
図**を理解し、追い返しました。彼女は、炎とのつながり

every evening, eagerly anticipating the enchanting spectacle. Maya's dances became a source of joy and wonder, bringing the community closer **together**. The dancing flames provided warmth not only to their bodies but also to their spirits. But as Maya's fame grew, so did envy and greed. Outsiders arrived, seeking to claim her power for themselves.

They offered riches and promises of grandeur, hoping to exploit her gift. Maya, wise beyond her years, recognized their **intentions** and turned them away. She understood that her connection with the flames was not for personal gain, but to bring light and happiness to others. Years passed, and Maya's dances continued to captivate hearts. The villagers regarded her as a guardian of their spirits, a **beacon** of hope in times of darkness. And as she gracefully swayed with the dancing flames, Maya knew that her gift was not just a talent but a **responsibility**. She would continue to nurture the flames' dance, sharing their warmth and enchantment with all who sought solace and joy. And so, in the small village nestled at the foot of the mighty mountain, Maya's dances with the dancing flames lived on, weaving a **tapestry** of magic and wonder that touched the souls of all who witnessed their enchanting beauty.

は個人的な利益のためではなく、人々に光と幸福をもたらすためであることを理解したのです。何年経っても、マヤの踊りは人々の心を魅了し続けました。村人たちは、マヤを精神の守護者、暗闇の中の希望の**光と見なしました**。そして、マヤは踊る炎と一緒に優雅に揺れながら、自分の才能が単なる才能ではなく、**責任であることを知った**。マヤは、自分の才能が単なる才能ではなく、責任を伴うものであることを知った。そして、マヤと炎のダンスは、山のふもとにある小さな村で、魔法と驚異の**タペストリーを**織り成し、その魅惑的な美しさを目にしたすべての人の魂に響くように生き続けた。

Comprehension
Questions

1. What was Maya's special gift?

2. How did Maya feel when she witnessed the dance of flames?

3. What made the flames seem different on the chilly evening?

4. How did Maya join the dance with the flames?

5. How did the villagers react to Maya's dances with the flames?

6. What did Maya understand about her connection with the flames?

7. Why did outsiders come to the village?

8. How did Maya respond to the offers from the outsiders?

9. How did the villagers perceive Maya?

10. What did Maya consider her responsibility regarding her gift?

理解度チェック問題

1. マヤの特別なプレゼントは何だったのでしょうか?
2. 炎の舞を目の当たりにしたマヤは、どのような気持ちになったのでしょうか。
3. 肌寒い夜、炎が違って見えたのはなぜ?
4. マヤはどのようにして炎とのダンスに参加したのでしょうか。
5. マヤの炎を使ったダンスに、村人たちはどう反応したのだろうか。
6. マヤは炎とのつながりをどう理解したのか。
7. なぜ部外者が村に来たのか?
8. マヤは部外者からの申し出にどう対応したのでしょうか。
9. 村人たちはマヤをどう捉えていたのでしょうか。
10. マヤは自分のプレゼントについて、どのような責任を考えていたのでしょうか。

Tangled Web

At the heart of the Tangled Web was Cassandra, a **mysterious** woman with flowing raven hair and eyes that held ancient wisdom. She was the master weaver, pulling the strings that connected the lives of the building's inhabitants. Cassandra knew everyone's secrets, their hopes, and their fears. She watched as the tangled web of human **existence** unfolded, delicately manipulating the threads to create unforeseen connections. Among the inhabitants of the Tangled Web was Michael, a **struggling** musician with dreams of fame. He found solace in the building's walls, pouring his heart and soul into each melody. Little did he know that his music had caught the attention of Ava, a troubled artist residing on the floor below. Ava, haunted by her own demons, found inspiration in Michael's **melodies**. Their chance encounter in the narrow hallway sparked a creative spark that would forever change their lives.

As their friendship blossomed, a love triangle began to take **shape**. Sarah, a vivacious dancer, had been entangled in a tumultuous relationship with Michael. Jealousy and **passion** intertwined, creating a complex web of emotions. Sarah, unaware of the connection between Ava and Michael, fought to

タングルドウェブ

カサンドラは、流れるようなレイヴンの髪と古代の知恵を秘めた瞳を持つ**ミステリアスな女性である**。彼女は、このビルの住人の人生をつなぐ糸を引く、織物の名手だった。カサンドラは皆の秘密、希望、そして恐怖を知っていた。彼女は人間**存在の**もつれた網が広がるのを見守り、糸を繊細に操って予期せぬつながりを作り出した。この "Tangled Web "の住人の一人であるマイケルは、名声を夢見る**苦労人のミュージシャンだった**。彼は、この建物の壁の中に安らぎを見出し、一つ一つのメロディに心を込めていた。しかし、その音楽が下の階に住むアーティストのエヴァの目に留まるとは知る由もなかった。マイケルの**メロディーは**、**自分**自身の悪魔に取り憑かれたアバにインスピレーションを与えるものだった。狭い廊下での偶然の出会いが、2人の人生を変えるクリエイティブな火種となった。

二人の友情が開花するにつれ、三角関係が**生まれ始めた**。快活なダンサーであるサラは、マイケルとの波乱に満ちた関係に絡め取られていた。嫉妬と**情熱が交錯し**、複雑な感情の網が張り巡らされていた。アバとマイケルの関係に気づかないサラは、離れていく**はずの愛にしが**みつこうと戦っていた。一方、"Tangled Web "の最上階では、アグネスという老女が毎日編み物をしていた。彼女の手は正確に動き、過去の糸から物語の**タペストリーを織り上げていく**。アグネスはこの建物の秘密を解く鍵を握っていた。彼女が記憶を解き明かすにつれ、住人たちの人生は永遠に変わっていった。

結局のところ、Tangled Webはその**目的を果たした**。そ

hold on to the love she **believed** was slipping away. Meanwhile, on the top floor of the Tangled Web, an elderly woman named Agnes spent her days knitting. Her hands moved with precision, weaving a **tapestry** of stories from the threads of her past. Agnes held the key to unlocking the secrets of the building, and as she unraveled her memories, the lives of the inhabitants were forever changed.

In the end, the Tangled Web had served its **purpose**. The lives of its inhabitants had become intricately woven together, bound by the choices they made and the consequences they faced. Love, betrayal, and redemption were all entwined in the threads of their **existence**. As the sun set on the Tangled Web, the old building stood as a testament to the complexity of human **relationships**. Its walls whispered stories of love lost and found, secrets revealed, and the fragile nature of the human heart. And within its tangled depths, the inhabitants continued to navigate the web of their lives, forever entwined in a **delicate** dance of fate and choice.

こに住む人々の人生は、複雑に織り込まれ、彼らが行った選択と直面した結果によって結ばれていた。愛と裏切り、そして贖罪が、彼らの**存在の**糸に絡み付いていた。その古い建物は、人間**関係の**複雑さを物語るかのように建っていた。その壁は、失われた愛と見つけた愛、明らかにされた秘密、そして人間の心のもろさを囁いている。そして、その奥深くで、住人たちは、運命と選択の**微妙なダンスの**中で永遠に絡み合いながら、人生の網の目を操り続けているのである。

Comprehension Questions

1. Who is the central character at the heart of the Tangled Web?

2. What is Cassandra's role in the building?

3. What does Cassandra know about the building's inhabitants?

4. How does Michael find solace in the Tangled Web?

5. Who is Ava and how is she connected to Michael?

6. What emotions are intertwined in the love triangle that forms?

7. How does Sarah feel about her relationship with Michael?

8. What is Agnes's role in the Tangled Web?

9. What does Agnes do with her time in the building?

10. How does the Tangled Web serve as a testament to the complexity of human relationships?

理解度チェック問題

1. Tangled Webの中心人物は誰でしょうか?
2. カサンドラの役割とは?
3. カサンドラはビルの住人について何を知っているのだろうか。
4. マイケルは「Tangled Web」の中でどのような慰めを得るのだろうか?
5. エヴァとは何者なのか、そしてマイケルとどのような関係があるのか。
6. 形成される三角関係には、どんな感情が絡み合うのでしょうか。
7. サラはマイケルとの関係をどう感じているのだろうか。
8. アグネスの「Tangled Web」での役割とは?
9. アグネスは館内で何をしているのでしょうか?
10. 人間関係の複雑さを物語る「Tangled Web」は、どのような役割を果たしているのでしょうか。

Silent Guardian

Generations had come and gone, but the villagers had grown
complacent, their belief in the Guardian's power fading
with time. They stopped leaving offerings and ceased to honor
the **traditions** passed down through the ages. Forgotten and
ignored, the Silent Guardian stood alone, its presence taken
for granted. One stormy night, as the villagers slept peacefully,
a band of thieves descended upon the village, their eyes set on
riches and treasures. They believed that the Silent Guardian
was nothing more than an old superstition. As they approached
the **statue**, their laughter filled the air, mocking the villagers'
belief in its protective powers. But as the thieves laid their hands
upon the statue, an eerie silence fell upon the village. The wind
ceased its howling, and the rain stopped its relentless **assault**. A
shiver ran down their spines as the Silent Guardian's stone eyes
seemed to glow with an otherworldly light.

Suddenly, a powerful gust of wind swept through the village,
knocking the **thieves** off their feet. They watched in terror
as the Silent Guardian's stone form came to life. With each
step, the **ground** trembled beneath its feet. The Guardian's
expression hardened, and its eyes blazed with determination.
The thieves tried to escape, but they were no match for the

サイレントガーディアン

何世代にもわたり、村人たちは**満足し**、ガーディアンの力に対する信念は時代とともに薄れていきました。村人たちは供え物を置くことをやめ、昔から受け継がれてきた**伝統に敬意**を払うこともしなくなりました。忘れ去られ、無視され、サイレントガーディアンは、その存在を当然のこととして、孤独に立ち尽くしていました。ある嵐の夜、村人たちが安らかに眠っていると、盗賊の一団が富と財宝を目当てに村に降りてきた。彼らは、サイレントガーディアンが単なる迷信に過ぎないと信じていた。村人たちが信じているその守護神をあざ笑うように、盗賊たちは**像に**近づくと、笑いがこみ上げてきた。しかし、盗賊たちが像に手をかけたとき、村に不気味な静寂が訪れた。風は止み、雨は止みました。そして、サイレント・ガーディアンの石の目が、この世のものとは思えないほどの光を放ち、村人たちの背筋は凍りつきました。

突然、強い突風が村に吹き荒れ、**盗賊たちは**足元をすくわれた。サイレント・ガーディアンの石造りの姿が浮かび上がるのを、彼らは恐怖の眼差しで見つめた。一歩一歩、**足元が**震える。ガーディアンの表情は硬くなり、その目は決意に燃えている。盗賊たちは逃げようとしたが、サイレント・ガーディアンの怒りには勝てない。優雅に、そして正確に動き回り、彼らの**心に**恐怖を与えていく。盗賊たちは次々と地面に倒れ、戦利品は散乱し、忘れ去られていった。夜が明けると、村人たちは危険のない村に目を覚ました。村人たちは、倒された盗賊と毅然としたサイレントガーディアンの姿に驚嘆した。それ

Silent Guardian's wrath. It moved with grace and precision, striking fear into their **hearts**. One by one, the thieves fell to the ground, their loot scattered and forgotten. As dawn broke, the villagers awoke to a village free from danger. They marveled at the sight before them—the defeated thieves and the resolute Silent Guardian. It was a reminder of the power and **protection** that had always been bestowed upon them.

From that day forward, the villagers treated the Silent Guardian with the **reverence** it deserved. They restored the traditions and honored the Guardian's presence. The village thrived under its **watchful** eye, and the legend of the Silent Guardian spread far and wide, inspiring neighboring villages to cherish their own protectors. The Silent Guardian, once forgotten, had become a symbol of **strength** and unity. And as it stood in the heart of the village, its eyes filled with pride, it silently vowed to continue its eternal vigil, forever the silent **protector** of the people it cherished.

は、いつも自分たちを守ってくれていた力を思い起こさせるものであった。

その日以来、村人たちはサイレントガーディアンに敬意をもって接するようになりました。村人たちは伝統を取り戻し、ガーディアンの存在に敬意を払った。そして、サイレントガーディアンの伝説は広く知られるようになり、近隣の村々も自分たちの守護神を大切にするようになりました。かつて忘れ去られていたサイレント・ガーディアンは、強さと結束の象徴となった。そして、サイレントガーディアンは、村の中心に立ち、その瞳を誇りに思いながら、静かにその永遠の警戒を続けることを誓った。

Comprehension Questions

1. Why did the belief in the Silent Guardian's power fade among the villagers over time?

2. What did the thieves think of the Silent Guardian?

3. What happened when the thieves laid their hands on the statue?

4. How did the Silent Guardian's appearance change when it came to life?

5. How did the thieves react when the Silent Guardian started moving?

6. What was the outcome of the encounter between the thieves and the Silent Guardian?

7. How did the villagers feel when they woke up after the encounter with the thieves?

8. What did the villagers do to show reverence and honor to the Silent Guardian after the incident?

9. How did the village thrive under the watchful eye of the Silent Guardian?

10. What did the Silent Guardian become for the villagers and neighboring villages?

理解度チェック問題

1. なぜ、時を経て、村人たちの間で「サイレントガーディアン」の力を信じる気持ちが薄れていったのでしょうか。

2. 盗賊たちは、サイレントガーディアンをどう思ったのでしょうか。

3. 泥棒が像に手をかけたらどうなったか?

4. サイレントガーディアンは、命を吹き込まれると、どのように姿が変わるのでしょうか?

5. サイレントガーディアンが動き出したとき、泥棒たちはどう反応したのでしょうか?

6. 盗賊とサイレントガーディアンの出会いは、どのような結末を迎えたのでしょうか?

7. 盗賊との出会いで目覚めた村人たちは、どんな気持ちだったのでしょうか。

8. 事件後、村人たちは「沈黙の守護者」に敬意と尊敬の念を示すために何をしたのでしょうか。

9. サイレント・ガーディアンの見守る中、村はどのように繁栄していったのだろうか。

10. 村人や近隣の村にとって、サイレントガーディアンはどんな存在になったのでしょうか。

Glass Slipper

Once upon a time, in a small village nestled deep in a lush **valley**, there lived a young girl named Ella. Ella was a dreamer who loved to lose herself in the pages of fairy tales. Her favorite story was about a **beautiful** princess who found her true love with the help of a magical glass slipper. Ella's days were filled with chores and mundane tasks, but she never lost hope that one day, her own fairy tale would unfold. Every evening, she would gaze at the stars, wishing for a bit of magic to change her life. One morning, as Ella was fetching water from the **village** well, she noticed a peculiar glimmer in the crystal-clear water. Curiosity overwhelmed her, and she bent down to get a closer look. Floating in the water was a delicate, shimmering glass slipper. Ella's heart leaped with **excitement**, believing her fairy tale was about to begin.

With trembling hands, she lifted the glass slipper from the **water** and held it to the sunlight. It was the most exquisite thing she had ever seen, delicate and sparkling like a star. Ella knew in her heart that this was no **ordinary** shoe. Determined to uncover the secrets behind the glass slipper, Ella embarked on a journey. She traveled to the kingdom's grand **palace**, where the royal ball was to take place. Word had spread far and wide

ガラスの靴

昔々、緑豊かな**谷の奥**にある小さな村に、エラという名の少女が住んでいました。エラは夢見がちで、おとぎ話の世界に入り込むのが大好きでした。エラの大好きなお話は、**美しいお姫様が魔法のガラスの靴で真実の愛を見つける**というものでした。エラの毎日は、雑用と平凡な仕事でいっぱいだったが、いつか自分のおとぎ話が展開されるという希望は失わなかった。毎晩、星空を眺めながら、自分の人生を変えてくれる魔法がないかと願った。ある朝、エラは**村の井戸で水を汲んでいると、澄んだ水の中に奇妙な輝きがあることに気づいた。好奇心旺盛なエラは、腰をかがめてよく見てみた。水面に浮いていたのは、繊細な輝きを放つガラスの靴でした。エラは、これからおとぎ話が始まるのだと、**胸を躍らせた。**

彼女は震える手でガラスの靴を**水面から持ち上げ**、陽の光にかざした。それは、今まで見たこともないような、繊細で星のような輝きを放つ優美なものだった。エラは、この靴が**普通の靴**ではないことを心の中で確信した。エラは、このガラスの靴に隠された秘密を明らかにしようと決意し、旅に出た。舞踏会が開かれる王国の**大宮殿へ**。王子は真実の愛を求めており、ガラスの靴を履いた者が王子の**心を射止める**という噂が広まっていた。

エラが宮殿の門に着くと、その謙虚な**姿に**、靴を試しに来た人たちから冷ややかな視線が注がれた。しかしエラは、それでもめげなかった。エラは気品と威厳をもって前に進み、ガラスの靴を王子に差し出しました。王子は固唾を飲んでエラの前にひざまずき、ガラスの靴を彼女の足にはかせました。すると、まるでエラのために作ら

that the prince sought his true love, and the one who fit the glass slipper would win his **heart**.

As Ella arrived at the palace gates, her humble **appearance** earned her scornful glances from the others who had come to try on the slipper. But Ella remained undeterred. With grace and dignity, she stepped forward, presenting the glass slipper to the prince. With bated breath, the prince knelt before Ella, slipping the glass slipper onto her foot. To everyone's **astonishment**, it fit perfectly, as if it were made for her. The prince looked into Ella's eyes and saw not just a girl with a glass slipper but a soul filled with kindness and **dreams**. Their love blossomed, and Ella's fairy tale became a reality. She discovered that the glass slipper was more than a symbol of a happily ever after; it was a testament to her unwavering belief in magic and her **willingness** to embrace her dreams.

れたかのように、ガラスの靴はぴったりとはまり、誰もが驚いた。王子はエラの目を見ると、ガラスの靴を履いただけの少女ではなく、優しさと夢でいっぱいの魂が見えました。そして、エラのおとぎ話は現実のものとなり、二人の愛は花開いた。エラは、ガラスの靴が単なる幸せの象徴ではなく、魔法を信じ、夢を抱きしめてきた証であることを知ったのです。

Comprehension Questions

1. What was the name of the young girl in the story?

2. What did Ella enjoy losing herself in?

3. What was Ella's favorite fairy tale about?

4. What did Ella hope would happen one day?

5. What did Ella notice in the crystal-clear water of the village well?

6. How did Ella feel when she saw the glass slipper in the water?

7. Where did Ella travel to in order to uncover the secrets behind the glass slipper?

8. What had spread far and wide regarding the prince?

9. How did others react to Ella's humble appearance at the palace gates?

10. What did the prince see in Ella's eyes when he looked at her?

理解度チェック問題

1. 物語に登場する少女の名前は何だったのでしょうか?
2. エラは何に没頭して楽しんでいたのでしょうか?
3. エラが好きだった童話は、どんな内容だったのでしょうか?
4. エラは、いつかこうなることを望んでいたのでしょうか。
5. エラは、村の井戸の澄んだ水を見て、何に気づいたのだろう。
6. 水の中にあるガラスの靴を見たとき、エラはどんな気持ちになったのでしょうか。
7. エラはガラスの靴に隠された秘密を解き明かすために、どこへ旅立ったのだろう。
8. 王子について、何が広く伝わっていたのか。
9. エラが宮殿の門に謙虚に現れたとき、他の人々はどのように反応したのでしょうか。
10. 王子はエラの目を見たとき、何を感じたのだろう。

Printed in Great Britain
by Amazon

29524226R00088